Top: 1997 - Claudia,remember me? - the return.
Middle: 1994 - The Leipzig skyline - cranes or TV aerials?
Bottom: 1994 - Sankt Elisabeth Krankenhaus, Leipzig.

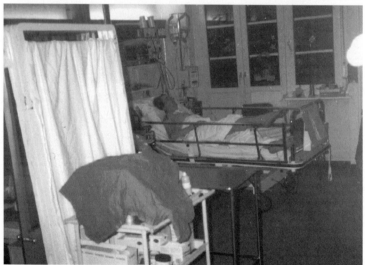

Top: That stairwell; myself, Terry and two paramedics are down there somewhere.
Bottom: Lying in intensive care, my home for a month.

Chapter Four

Time for a Break

A weekend of solid World Cup viewing took us straight into week two on the job, and our first task on Monday morning was to skive off for an hour. With our trip home getting ever nearer, we had to decide how we would travel and pay for it. We had vowed never to stray within a mile of a train after our adventures on day one, and our finances did not make flying a viable proposition. We could afford it, but it would take a huge chunk out of what would appear from our wallets upon our reunions with our respective partners. Nobody we knew who had travelled by car was to return home around the time that we were due to vanish, and so the final option would have to do.

Sitting on a coach for twenty-four hours was not a prospect to look forward to, but what the hell, we were going home. I would have been happy to crawl. No matter how good the work was, how much money you were earning or how many mates you had, you always wanted to go home. Few of us wanted to be there in the first place and if a decent job back home had offered itself to us, not many would have refused it and stayed abroad. I was most definitely one of them. Terry felt the same way and neither of us gave a toss how Roger felt. The tickets were paid for and back to the real world we would be heading, so we started to throw walls and ceilings up at a quite phenomenal rate, absolutely determined to have our wallets as full as possible before we left for a much-needed break.

The banter on the site was starting to become heated in a friendly way as the following day Germany was to play in the World Cup against the might of Bulgaria! Every scoreline involving Germany losing was daubed on the walls of the building. Our German colleagues were taking the light-hearted ribbing in the way it was intended – as a joke. The majority of the Germans that we had met had been helpful, welcoming and appreciative of us being there. The full extent of their football-related hostilities revolved around working out what the English was for, 'At least we qualified.' A friendly attitude that I was to experience, albeit on a higher plane, in a mere three months' time.

For the first time in days we made lengthy phone calls. Lucy apologised for the abrupt tone of her letter, but made it clear that cash and not my well-being was her number one priority.

Meanwhile, outside the site a van with a 'GB' sticker had appeared. Either someone had splashed out on some transport or we had some new arrivals. It turned out to be the latter. Their allotted workspace had been hurriedly arranged and they had been placed at the entrance to the building. As soon as we returned from our trip to the nearest telephone kiosk, introductions were made. The two new lads appeared to be cold, very dirty and it wasn't to be too long before the fact that they were almost starving to death entered the conversation. Jack and Pete had been in the country for three days and had been forced to sleep in their van. Prior to their arrival they had been working back at the same site where we had started our campaign and then left in such a hurry.

Two and two made four – they had answered the very same advert that Terry had enquired about. Mr Smarm had obviously worked at speed to replace us and found two more builders to snare in his financial web.

For them it was still very early days and they talked at length about how content they were with the work they had. Sure they hadn't been paid yet, but the agent had promised them that he would send money home to their wives to help them through until they had their first wage safely tucked in their back pockets. Terry glanced across the room and gave me a knowing look. We knew it would not be too long before all the promises proved to be false and all the expectancy surrounding what they hoped to achieve from their work in Germany would come crashing down around their work boots.

With Jack and Pete working on the same site as Terry and myself, it would not be too long before our path crossed with that of our ex-agent again. Maybe we could reveal the truth and talk some sense into the new lads before his arrival. It would all depend on whether they would believe our stories or see them as the tales of two bitter employees. If it was to be the latter, it would be one hell of a shock when the truth finally dawned. We'd been there, seen it, done it, and bought the scruffy T-shirt.

We had two guests at our table that night and no excuses for not tipping the waiter needed to be made up as to add to Jack's woes, a tray of drinks found its way on to his lap as our hapless beige-suited attendant stumbled on the shag pile. The end of a very bad day for Jack, but a hysterical moment for us and indeed the rest of the diners. As our companions were not employed by the same company that had the agreement with the hotel, no cheap rooms could be found for them. They could however, join us in our room for use of the bathing facilities they badly needed. Three days of dust and sweat had to be removed, along with the contents of four bottles of beer off the waiter's tray.

We returned to our room just in time to turn on the television and witness Germany being knocked out of the World Cup. As the final whistle blew, a huge cheer rang out from the British contingent in the hotel, loud enough to pass on the result to Jack standing in the shower, oblivious to anything other than the hot soapy water. It was either going to be jokes aplenty the next day or we would all be beaten senseless, as our German friends tired of what would inevitably be endless ribbing.

Jack finally emerged from the bathroom and took a seat next to us to enjoy the comfort of a hotel room before he would have to depart and make his way down to the car park for another night in the back of his van. We felt no guilt at all regarding his and Pete's situation. It was almost as if we were treating it as their initiation into the harsh realities of Brits making their way and trying to earn a living in another country. We had been forced to undergo that ceremony on two occasions, in two different train stations, so we were not going to feel any sympathy for any workers who turned up with the comfort of a ten-year-old van to fall back on. Luxury!

After hanging around in our room for as long as they possibly could to avoid spending any more time out in the cold than they had to, Jack and Pete finally departed around midnight. Terry left close behind to make his way to a telephone to use the small amount of money he had. I cracked open another bottle of beer and settled back down in my chair, and Roger? Well, for all I knew he could have been burning the rest of the hotel down. I had long since ceased paying attention to, or caring about what he was doing.

The big white van was still in the car park next morning as we left the hotel on our way back to the site. Jack and Pete would probably have had an uncomfortable night's sleep in the van. So what? Constant and vigorous hammering on the vehicle's side soon aroused them from whatever state of unconsciousness they were in. It was only fair that all our generosity of the night before should be repaid by having a lift to the site, depriving us of the dubious pleasure of travelling by tram.

A not so pleasant surprise awaited us at the site: a very familiar mobile home sat outside the building, the very same van Mr Smarm was forced to sleep in, with shower, electricity, TV and all mod cons – a very different scenario to Jack and Pete's. Out of the mobile palace he leapt with his usual grinning face that you wanted to punch – badly! We were not the first to be stolen from his grasp by our new employers and so he would be keeping a close eye on his new recruits while they fraternised with the enemy. With so many individuals competing for the same work in such a small area, it was important that each agent hung on to as many of his workers as possible. No work, no commission, might as well go home, simple.

The greeting to Jack and Pete was short and then he made his way over in our direction to inform us that things were not sorted out regarding the fire. Flimsy threats intended to be frighteners followed, didn't have the required impact and were duly ignored. Unknown to him, we had already heard on the building site grapevine that he was, in fact, intending to buy the unit himself, thereby acquiring even cheaper accommodation which he would, no doubt, rent out to his minions for an extortionate amount to line his pockets even more.

The routine of sleep, work, sleep, work, with the occasional trip to the land of alcohol had become a way of life and the days were starting to pass with monotonous regularity. But yet again a slap in the face was looming on the horizon. Since we had arrived at the hotel, another ten men from the company with nowhere to stay had been instructed to check in. The agreement was in place that more heads meant cheaper bills. It wasn't unfair for us to expect our bill to be a little smaller. It didn't drop by a single pfennig and hadn't done so since Terry, Roger and myself had arrived. The management were well pleased, but the expats were restless. The agreement had been the idea of the hotel management and we had all made the mistake of trusting and believing. The entire British quarter of the hotel synchronised watches and agreed to meet in the reception area for a friendly discussion. A speaker was elected back at the site and on everyone's behalf, a well-rehearsed ultimatum was delivered to the man in charge on our return to the hotel that night. He sat and listened as our speaker reeled off our half-threat, half-bluff: if the bill had not been lowered by the morning, we would all up and go. Twenty men paying twenty bills adds up to one large sum of money – too much to risk losing. They would surely panic, agree to our demands and we would all happily stay put?

As we all packed our bags to leave the following morning we took turns to embrace our best friend, the TV set. All the time a certain amount of anger was building up caused by the pack of lies that the hotel management had told us. It was payback time, an unfortunate phrase for the event that followed. Every British alarm clock had been synchronised and set to rouse us all early enough to avoid anyone at the reception desk. Full use was made of Jack's van as numerous trips were made to fill it with everybody's baggage and that was that – off we went. No payment, and most certainly no forwarding address. Strictly speaking, not the most friendly way to deal with things, but we had played their game and they had cheated. If their fairness had continued we would all have happily paid our bills and put more custom their way. It was their loss.

Two of the lads spent the day searching for new digs, finally coming good at 7 p.m. as we were about to leave work. Four men would be expected to fill each room, so Terry and I agreed to share with Jack and Pete who had become sick of sleeping in the back of that van. There was no agreement involving our employers with the owners of these flats and as Jack and Pete were no longer the outsiders, they jumped at the chance of living in a room that didn't have wheels. Nobody cared who was working for whom; as long as they paid their share of the bill, anyone was welcome.

The luxuries of living in the hotel that we had just left seemed a distant memory as we entered our new abode. Each flat was virtually a squat compared to what we had just left behind. A kitchen, bathroom and two bedrooms – end of story. No restaurant and more importantly, no access to a television set. Soon after entering the flat, the process began of deciding who slept where. Two bedrooms with two beds in each made four beds, easy. Then Roger entered the equation – damn, we'd forgotten him! Terry and I paid his wages and Jack and Pete would kick the shit out of him if they were left bedless. Fortunately for Roger a couch sat in the corner of our room and so he did at least have something to lie upon.

After a quick meal in our new surroundings, it was time to leave the flat and search the locality for anything of interest to a builder in a foreign land coming home after a hard day's work. A five-minute walk and – bingo! We soon stumbled across a good old-fashioned traditional English pub tucked away on the outskirts of Leipzig to cater for the needs of every Brit living in the vast complex of flats that we were calling home. All of a sudden the lack of a television set to while away the hours didn't seem half as bad as it had ten minutes before our reconnaissance mission. So far we had only seen our quarter of the complex and a tiny quarter it was. There were, in fact, almost two hundred Brits living in the area, a new group of contacts for possible work and just plain and simple drinking pals. But the British were not the only nationally found in the area. At regular intervals Mongolians would spring out of the woodwork grasping cartons of cigarettes and gallons of alcohol that they intended to sell to the Brits at less than half the price that we would pay at any of the watering holes or shops in the area. That particular part of the city must have been a happy hunting ground as there was never a shortage of takers for their either smuggled or stolen goods. We never asked, and we never cared.

It was not only in the capacity of illegal street vendors that we were to come into contact with the Mongolians. A close look at any of the numerous building sites revealed many of their kind working as labourers, cleaners – in fact any job at all that would pay them a pittance. Terry and I intended to work for no more than five weeks at a time before returning home for a break; they were forced to stay for months at a time. Once they had arrived, they had little choice but to stay until they could return home with enough money to feed their families and that would only be if they could make enough money to pay for the journey as well. As far as the German workers were concerned, they were the lowest of the low. They were so desperate for work, they would happily work for scandalously low wages and were treated accordingly.

Their luck would not change after the day's work had finished either. Numerous hard-working Mongolians ended up hospitalised after violent attacks whilst trying to off-load their mobile off-licences. A chance to work on a site with the Brits made a pleasant change for them. They worked very hard and we treated them fairly in return. Ironically, in repayment for their hard graft, we would lavish upon them the same cigarettes and cans of beer that we had bought from their mates the night before. We were all stuck in a foreign land and appreciated their efforts that were only punctuated by harrowing stories of their families that they had left behind. These tales really put into perspective our respective situations and concerns.

By the final week of tour number one we had eased into a routine of working on the site all day then heading to the English pub to get extremely friendly with whoever had been bothered to walk to the newsagent and purchase an English newspaper, eventually attempting to get him pissed so that he wouldn't know who we were and therefore wouldn't notice the newspaper disappearing.

The final day on the site felt like a week. At long last, tour number one had come to an end.

Chapter Five

Down to Earth – With a Bang

Escaping from the site on our final day was virtually impossible. It was traditional that whenever a colleague was due to leave for a break back in Britain, he would be surrounded by his fellow workers who would all brandish shopping lists of all the luxuries they were missing and expected to be brought back with them. Ten lists containing such items as cheddar cheese, butter, bacon, soft toilet rolls and, last but not least, nubile young women, were thrust into our hands and we finally got away. Prior to leaving we had been made to promise that we would bring back all the items to Germany with us – a promise that we had been happy to make while knowing full well it would be forgotten as soon as we arrived back home.

There would be no farewell drinks at the bar that night, as the coach was due to set off at five a.m. to begin our arduous thirty-six-hour journey back to Blighty. Immediately after yet another huge meal, Terry, Roger and myself retired for what would have to be a good night's sleep – an impossible feat. We felt too much like children on Christmas Eve with our minds fixed firmly on seeing friends and family and eating meat that had actually been cooked.

As morning broke, Jack started to regret driving over in his van. He had made the hideous mistake of promising to give us a lift to the station. When your promise has to be carried out before the sun has risen, all of a sudden you aren't quite the friend you thought you were. Jack finally arose after five minutes of verbal abuse.

It was only after all our baggage had been thrown into his van that it began to sink in that we were actually going home. The copious amounts of *coffee* that had been drunk began to kick in and we were just happy to be alive. It took leaving the bloody country to bring about this state of euphoria.

Like most of the world, Germany's roads are relatively empty at that time of day and so our journey to the station was a short one. On arriving at the station it was a surprise to find that we were the only builders waiting to board the coach, and for that matter only two Germans would be joining us also. We had expected the coach to be full and so it was when it finally arrived, half an hour late. Leipzig was only a pick-up point for the coach on the route from Dresden. There had obviously been a far greater demand for seats there as only five remained for us to choose from. But first we had to load our baggage on to the coach.

As we searched for the driver, we ignored a strange-smelling long-haired individual making weird grunting noises and carried on our search. Unfortunately, the unwashed, toothless man that we had just passed *was* the driver and he proceeded to roughly throw our bags on to the coach. Terry and I then had the choice of either sitting with Roger or choosing instead the two seats next to the werewolf with the driving licence. It was no contest. He spoke not a word of English and the smell was unbearable, yet he was still infinitely better company than Roger whom we had grown to despise almost murderously.

As we sat back in our seats and relaxed, I wished that the coach wouldn't stop until we reached London. However, the first of many stops made by the coach was in Jena two hours away from Leipzig, and by coincidence the only passenger to board the coach was an Englishman returning from a holiday. Terry and myself now had someone other than Roger to communicate with on the remainder of our trek home.

Roger now seemed to sense that he was now the outcast that we had always seen him as. If only reality had dawned sooner. The only thing he had done during the whole stay had been to successfully enable everyone around him to make his life a misery. Our financial situation would have been that much better if Roger had understood his utter uselessness soon after his arrival, and for him his journey had turned out to be a huge waste of his time and money. Good!

Time passed so much more quickly with a fresh face to talk to and have a laugh with. All of our horror stories were told and by the time we reached Brussels our now-found friend had grown to dislike Roger almost as much as we did.

A fifteen-minute stop at a roadside diner wasn't really an adequate amount of time to see the sights of the entire city. As we climbed back on to the coach I realised that we were in Belgium and hadn't once removed our passports from our pockets, but before I had time to discuss it with Terry the journey began again. Our next stop would be Ostend on the coast of Belgium where we would board our ferry.

The tiresome road trip came to an end as we at last reached Ostend. Looking out of the window of a coach in total darkness, Ostend isn't much to look at. The driver was clearly having problems finding his way as he stopped and parked the coach next to a raft, okay a large raft, but a raft all the same. After disembarking from the coach, closer inspection revealed that the raft with a bar and a toilet in the centre of it was actually the ferry that was to take us back to England – not the most luxurious ferry I had seen.

Our overnight voyage was spent in the bar as there was nowhere else other than the toilet. The floor of a ferry bar was still a luxury compared to some of our makeshift beds of the past few weeks. The only discomfort we had to suffer that night was the indignity of occasionally being trodden on by an unstable drinker with double vision in a hurry to leave the bar. However, it was going to take something more serious than that to upset us. We were only hours away from walking through our respective front doors and reacquainting ourselves with the delights of home. After tour number one it really was a relief to be having a break. Tour two would be easy; all of the learning had been done and the examinations were over. Now we knew what to expect. Our eyes were open, as opposed to squinting through the smoke and train fumes.

As the sun rose we all stood on the deck and watched the ferry pull into the harbour. Docking procedures are always painfully slow, multiplied tenfold when all you want to do is get off the vessel. After a long wait, the call finally came for us to return to our coach. Continuing the vein of carelessness that had dogged us throughout this trip, we had unfortunately failed to note which of the coaches aboard the ferry was ours. We stumbled incompetently around the parking area and as a search party was just being organised, Roger spotted the destination board. So he proved at last to be of some use, an hour before he disappeared for ever, to the delight of his companions.

A chorus of friendly cheers greeted our late arrival and the coach left the ferry and drove on to English soil. The temptation to dash off the coach and kiss the ground Pope style was resisted to save time. Surely there was nothing left to slow us down now? Dream on – we should have known better!

Even when totally innocent, a sight tinge of fear and guilt always manifests itself when being confronted by a customs officer. The passengers on our coach seemed to be having problems looking innocent as two aggressive-looking officers strolled threateningly up and down the length of the vehicle. No matter how hard you try, a guilty look always appears when you are desperately trying to look innocent. In an airport it is very easy to forget about the officers and calmly walk past them, but when you are sitting for twenty minutes only inches from the officer who is repeatedly walking past you and glaring, you begin to feel uncomfortable, even though you possess no more than a bag of dirty work clothes.

Then came the results of their intimidation tactics. One man seated towards the rear of the coach had either failed to appear innocent or confessed his guilt to smuggling. At least smuggling was one of the numerous possibilities that the rest of the passengers imagined was the reason for his ejection, along with theft, murder or even being a suspected Nazi war criminal, despite appearing to be no more than twenty years old. One of these outrageous stories may well have been true, as we never saw the startled suspect again. Were the two suitcases taken along with him concealing undesirable luggage as far as Customs and Excise were concerned? I couldn't really care less, as twenty minutes had been wasted sitting motionless awaiting his removal. Lock the bastard up and throw away the key was perhaps a touch uncharitable, but nonetheless probably how the rest of the passengers felt too.

In comparison to the rest of the long and tiring nine-hundred-mile journey, the trip from the harbour to London was a relatively short haul. As with any journey, no matter how great the distance, the nearer you get to your destination, the slower the wheels seem to turn and sheer boredom took a hold shortly after hitting the road. I took the chance to close my eyes and spent the final leg of the trip catching up on the sleep that had been disturbed at regular intervals by the soles of those drunkards' boots back on the ferry only hours before.

The coach shuddered to a halt and the first thing I saw when I woke from my short sleep was Victoria Coach Station. Farewells were exchanged with anyone who could understand English and we left the coach to hijack the first taxi that came into our view. Ten ecstatically happy minutes later we were stood inside a train station with no intention of sleeping there, just on going home.

It was time for Roger to at long last disappear back to wherever he had come from. Terry and I were going to have a great deal of difficulty keeping our emotions in check when it came to seeing Roger on to his train.

A look at the timetable told us that Roger's train would depart first and so the three of us found the platform. Terry and I stood aside while Roger boarded and then watched and waved as the train vanished into the distance. Our emotions did indeed build up until finally reaching a joyous crescendo of laughter. We were still laughing ten minutes later on the adjacent platform when our train arrived. Our bags were quite literally thrown into the carriage, seats taken and we were an hour away from home.

I had been very wrong about the length of the trip so far. The coach, the ferry and the countless stops had, in the scheme of things, lasted for only a few minutes but our train home was to take a millennium. Eventually the train stopped, we stepped down and finally stopped moving for the first time since climbing on to the coach back in Leipzig.

'Afternoon, mate. Been anywhere nice?' asked the taxi driver as I took my place in the back of his cab. My silence spoke volumes as we trundled up to Lucy's house for the long-awaited reunion. Being back in familiar surroundings was great and by the time Lucy's house appeared, a smile had replaced my grimace of the past six weeks.

A smiling face greeted me on the doorstep but was destined not to last for very long. The subject of money brought a swift end to the niceties within a minute of entering the house. My wallet appeared, to be met by a decidedly frosty reception as Lucy noticed immediately how thin it seemed. I launched into a long and detailed account of the reasons for the disappointing lack of funds.

The subdued atmosphere took a full hour to disperse and the expected happy reunion never really materialised. It may well have been a lot more cheerful than I remember, but the scenario that followed after the first smiling greeting soured everything that followed it, in my mind at least. Hindsight is a marvellous thing as events in the near future would teach me – painfully.

You really have to be a hundred per cent certain of anything that you intend to do and, more importantly, have the same degree of faith in the people that you choose to be close to. Even the slightest doubt puts you on perilously thin ice. Only very few get to complete their life and step off the rink with a perfect six. The rest trip and fall with a very real danger of falling on the ice and getting hurt. Sometimes the risks just aren't worth taking. Unfortunately, there are times when you refuse to believe that you are taking anything other than the easy route, despite glaring signs that point in the opposite direction.

Eventually, Lucy did apologise for her behaviour in a not very convincing manner and I chose to overlook it and smile gratefully. The rest of the day was spent travelling from house to house to visit my friends and family who were genuinely pleased to see me and wanted to hear all of the adventures we had unintentionally endured.

The first day of any return from the building sites is always tricky. The initial task is to shed the site habit of foul language, crude behaviour and just basic laddishness – a difficult enough job at home after spending eight hours working in that environment and almost impossible after exposure to it for twenty-four hours a day over a duration of six weeks. Two days of normality, however, is all it takes to reacclimatise yourself and by the time you are ready to leave again you are just as depressed at the prospect as you were when approaching tour number one.

Countless trips to the local watering hole and one or two meals with Lucy took me through the first week of my fourteen-day sabbatical. The remaining seven days were to be a much quieter affair, a whole week of restful days sat with my feet up, recuperating before returning to the lunacy over the water. What delights would this next trip have in store for us? Our initial stay had been eventful, to say the least.

Lucy's annoyance at the lack of any substantial money and my own annoyance about it, as well as with Lucy herself, were put aside for one night, as I prepared to return, reluctantly, the following morning. Joined by friends and relatives, the inevitable piss-up started early in the evening. Maybe it was not a sensible way of forgetting what was to come, but a successful one all the same. Not even the smallest part of me had any desire to make the return journey and most certainly not by the same never-ending coach route.

I said all my fond farewells again at the end of the night. We were only to be out of the country for four weeks this time, so it didn't seem quite so bad as it had before leaving for the first time. Lucy again gave me the impression that she wasn't unduly upset at the thought of my departure. I left with just a peck on my cheek and a touch perplexed by her lack of emotion. The next day it was left to my brother and sister-in-law to wave me off at the station and they were soon disappearing into the distance as the train rolled on to London where we would meet that bloody coach!

As soon as we had boarded the coach we realised that the return trip was to be even more tedious as we now knew that there was absolutely nothing at all to look forward to for the next thirty-six hours. We took the ferry crossing in our stride, by now almost seasoned sailors. Conversation was strangely muted during the more boring parts of the journey, until we realised that not having Roger tagging along like a lost puppy gave us nobody to take the piss out of. So everyone else on the coach got the treatment instead, naturally of course under our breaths so as not to be heard; there were only two of us and thirty of them!

Brussels and the rest of Belgium slipped by unnoticed and the rest of the journey was taken up with a routine of listen to tape, cigarette, toilet, listen to tape, etc. until – Leipzig again. We boarded the tram to our digs and spent the ten-minute run rehearsing all the reasons for not bringing back a single item of the shopping list given to us by the impatient masses. We had no bacon, no butter, no toilet rolls, and instead were concealing our own little stash of luxuries.

The first people to greet us back at the digs were Sheffield's answer to the Bee Gees. Three men – one thin, one with bouffant hair and one saddled with a high-pitched voice. When you are trying to pass time away on a building site, sometimes the area changes into something closely resembling a primary school playground with everyone having their own silly nickname – very, very childish, yet amusing if you are part of it.

Robin, Barry and Maurice were with us when we were working back at Mr Smarm's domain and were still just earning enough to stay afloat. Jack and Pete had told them of the flats that we were all living in and they had decided to try their luck with the owners, succeeded and started to rent a place of their own. It was like one big happy family, although not quite so big, as we found out after having a chat with the singing trio.

Jack and Pete had continued to work for their and our friend, while we had been enjoying our break back home.

We had tried to warn them of the possibilities of what might happen if they started to trust the slippery so-and-so, but they chose not to heed our warnings. Their pay day had arrived and the amount received was less than half what they had been expecting. Following close behind the cash, a new set of prices had been thrust upon them by the less than honest agent. Enough was enough. Their tools had been thrown into the van along with all of their baggage and a very early return home had been their only option. The by now almost universally hated agent had been in a local bar on the night of their departure and returned to his mobile home to find not a single window intact and all four tyres deflated on his precious vehicle. Coincidence? If it hadn't been – good! He had had it coming and much celebration ensued. At long last someone had had the nerve to do what numerous people including Terry and myself had wanted to do. Had it been Jack and Pete who had done the dirty deed? We would never know, as they seemed to have disappeared off the face of the earth.

After half an hour back at our now half-empty flat, an overwhelming urge for welcome-back trotter burgers swept over us. We were back in Germany all right! The English pub around the corner was to be our first port of call in order to wash down the mock meat that we had just consumed and to catch up on any earth-shattering events that we may have missed. Glasses were raised as we entered the establishment, quickly followed by their contents heading our way when we admitted that we had forgotten the bacon, coffee, toilet rolls etc. After drying off, it wasn't long before we caught up with everything that had gone on in our absence. There was no news but the obligatory stories of non-payment that always ended in a long-drawn-out chase ending at a non-existent office, where there would inevitably be no trace of life, let alone money.

Our first day back at work was to prove tiring as we tried desperately to fit back into the old routine, but unsuccessfully. The inside of the building that we had been working on was beginning to take shape and now the emphasis had switched to getting the outside of the building looking more like the twentieth century and less like a large squat. The brickwork was crumbling, window and doorframes were rotting and not one square inch of plaster remained. Restoring the place to an acceptable standard was going to be a massive job and so once again the Germans telephoned Britain and announced their need for a whole platoon of stonemasons on the double.

What luck! There was a group of ten of the said tradesmen coming to the end of a similar job only an hour's drive away. Two days later they arrived and simply took over the entire building. They were very difficult to avoid, and the whole place was to be covered from top to bottom in scaffolding to enable all of the work to be done. The plastering was to be a long-drawn-out process, giving the masons ample opportunity to wander around the building introducing themselves and generally getting in the way of anyone who was still working. Not many of us needed much of an excuse to stop working for five minutes. The first mason who we met informed us that they had all been in the country for a whole year and were therefore eleven months more confident than Terry and myself.

The stonemasons continued on their quest to familiarise themselves with everyone on the site throughout the time it took to erect the scaffolding, all five floors of it. The business of erecting the scaffolding was an incredibly noisy and lengthy process that was not easy to ignore. Yet we managed, and we didn't have a great deal of choice. We could either carry on and receive our wages and a migraine or stop and receive nothing, nothing other than a slap in the face from our loved ones on our next return home.

The new influx of bodies on the site had given us the chance to get to know a whole new circle of contacts. Jack and Pete had gone so the new faces came at exactly the right time. It was a case of getting to know them all and weeding out the bad from the good. It was soon apparent that the masons had provided us with the usual widespread collection of characters to add to the motley crew who were already assembled in the building. Their team was to be completed later in the week with the late arrival of two more men, Paul and George.

With all the new boys on the site, work became almost enjoyable. The first two or three days after their arrival slipped by without event until... I had almost forgotten what it felt like, but another slap was winging its way in our direction. On our return to the digs after work, a handwritten note pushed under the door was waiting for us. There was an identical handwritten note lying on the welcome mat of every apartment being rented to the British workers residing there. All of the occupants were asked to pay up in full any outstanding rent owing to the landlords. In the time that we had stayed there, we had never had a single problem with either the landlord or the apartment itself. Having no reason to suspect that anything was amiss we all made a beeline to the office and happily paid up in full.

At the English pub that night rumours had begun to circulate regarding a group of eight fellow foreigners who had frequented the establishment every night of their stay. Their work had dried up and that night they were conspicuous by their absence. We had all learned to spot potential problems from the outset and their non-appearance that night led us all to believe that they had left the area pretty damned quickly. The landlord's odd behaviour was telling us that the builders who had disappeared had seen fit to let everyone else pay for their bad luck by leaving the country with their outstanding rent still just that –

outstanding. It's always the same, a small minority ruining it for everyone else. The landlord couldn't make the remaining Brits pay financially and instead he chose to make our lives difficult by throwing us all out, no warning, no fuss, goodbye. The Brits who had left had cost us all a home and we had to pay the price, something about tarring with a brush. Therefore he had decided to punish everyone by taking our rent while all the time intending to throw us out the next day.

Packing my bags was starting to really annoy me. I was doing it more often than I was eating a decent meal. On that particular occasion, all of our belongings were carted off to a housing agency in the city centre. That proved to be a fruitless venture as, ironically, the influx of masons on our site had taken up all the accommodation that was on offer. Two weeks earlier we would have been fine.

If you work for twelve hours a day in the same room with the same person, you soon get to know them quite well. Two or three hours is usually enough to give you a rough idea of what type of associate he is going to be in the future. Two or three days and you begin to tire. Two or three weeks you are ready for a fresh face to communicate with.

Trev was one of the more sociable members of the plastering team that were hard at it on the exterior of the building. At any one time their workforce always appeared to the untrained eye to be one man short. This was due to the phenomenon of each man on the site having now and then an uncontrollable urge to stop work and move away from his workplace for a break from prying eyes, to simply sit down and socialise with the rest of the men stuck out there with him. Put in simple terms, 'have a skive' became a well-worn phrase.

Trev's own particular brand of skiving was to leap from the scaffolding through the window of whichever room

Terry and myself were working in at that time. A flask would soon appear, along with a permanently half-empty packet of cigarettes and the conversation would soon turn to laughter. After a week of his impromptu visits, Trev had become one of our more trusted colleagues. On that particular day, the subject of our lack of accommodation soon reared its ugly head. Although by then it had become almost second nature to have the prospect of no place to lay our heads, it was still worrying us. Trev explained to us that on his arrival with his workmate, Paul, he had paid a visit to the very same housing agency that had recently wiped the last semblance of a smile off our distraught faces. Unlike us, they had been placed in a comfortable two-bedroomed flat with a bathroom, kitchen and a large sitting room, with two easy chairs and a large couch. Five minutes later a verbal contract was agreed between us and Terry and myself had somewhere to stay until we could find our own flat. It was a much appreciated gesture, an example of the 'look after our own' mentality that existed at the time. However, if anyone mentioned money the mood soon changed. Terry and I thanked Trev and Paul for their generosity with a promise of the drinks being on us for the duration of that night's funfest. Eventually work commenced again and we saw out the rest of the day in a slightly less depressed mood than the one in which we had started it.

Although the flat was only a brisk walk away, Trev and Paul still commuted by car and so Terry and I joined them at the end of the day, climbing into the car for the ninety-second drive to the flat. The flight of stairs leading up to our temporary accommodation seemed to get steeper the further up we went. Maybe a raging hunger and intense tiredness were contributory factors on our first day there. Was it all in our minds? The simple answer was yes, as all feelings of tiredness disappeared on opening the door. Trev confirmed that the metal box under the television set was indeed a satellite receiver beaming British TV programmes to the flat. We were then led into the kitchen and we saw a cooker that actually worked, the first we had seen since the infamous episode of the chip pan fire.

After eating a culinary miracle whipped up quickly by Paul, Trev began to explain exactly why our stay could only be temporary. Despite having a wife at home, he was working on a young lady he had met the previous week and, anticipating success, didn't fancy the prospect of having two builders wandering in very late at night, probably pissed and disturbing his privacy in an embarrassing way. He was taking things for granted and becoming over-confident, we thought. There was a possibility he would get let down badly and fall flat on his face.

Sure enough, before we knew it, Trev's potential relationship had got nowhere. Two weeks passed by with Terry and I still happily camping in his front room. The search for our own abode had progressed no further than Trev's sex life had, partly due to our liking of the comforts available to us in Trev's flat.

The end of the next working week coincided with the arrival of George, the final member of the plastering team. He shook everybody's hand, introduced himself and proceeded to talk non-stop for the rest of his stay, or so it seemed. It was soon clear that he had the sort of personality you would like to be blessed with yourself. He had the ability to strike up an instant rapport with virtually everyone he came into contact with.

George had only been on the site for twelve hours and had become friends with almost everybody, when we decided to introduce him to the friendly staff at the coffee house that we had all frequented numerous times every day. George's presence and the boisterous good-natured behaviour that ensued led to one of the girls who served us inviting all the Brits on site over to her home that evening to sample her home-cooked German cuisine, a show of friendliness that was accepted gladly. After our initial amazement at this show of friendliness we set about whittling down the fifteen Brits to an acceptable amount, finally setting on a total of six. Then we compiled a list of bottles of wine to be purchased, travel arrangements and the pub where we would all meet.

Work was finished a little earlier than usual to enable us all to make some sort of effort to look smart and we met up about two hours later in the pre-arranged watering hole. The conversation revolved around the unlikelihood of any of us back in Britain inviting six total strangers from another country to our house for a meal and to meet the wife. We all agreed that it was a show of friendship none of us would have even considered.

A big sloppy kiss was awaiting us all on arrival, along with the almost painfully firm handshake that the Germans were all so good at, from her husband. After a beer, a delicious meal was temptingly laid out buffet-style in front of us. Due to the eating habits that we all had acquired, this feast went down in record time, followed very quickly by the largest assortment of alcoholic goodies ever assembled in one home. As the conversation grew ever more drunken, it was revealed that her husband was named Seigfried, a touch confusing as her name was Seigried. When you are very inebriated, remembering who has no 'f' in their name becomes a bit tricky, so Seaweed was born and she didn't seem at all bothered, certainly not the next day when we arrived with a huge bunch of flowers to thank her for the incredible hospitality shown to us.

Another trip home was looming and Trev was at last beginning to make progress with his fancy piece. Because of this, yet more new digs had to be found and quickly, as we didn't wish to return to nothing, which was looking increasingly likely.

Lunchtime the following day was spent on our usual chairs outside Seaweed's café, just passing time. All of a sudden a cheer went up from all the girls in the vicinity, but mostly from Seaweed and her pals. There on top of the scaffolding outside the building we were working on, fully four storeys up, George was dancing and singing with his back to us and his arse gleaming in the sunlight. The girls were now pointing and moving their hands in a circular motion. George happily took the bait and turned round. Ten minutes later he joined us, arriving to cheers from Seaweed's pals as he entered the café like a triumphant gladiator. Needless to say, it was a different matter with the blokes. Maggot drawers, pin pricks and chippolata were to name but three of the comments we made!

Before working on our site, the plasterers had been working about fifty miles away in Magdeburg, spending their spare time in a local nightclub and becoming very friendly with the owner and resident DJ. Terry and myself decided to sample this pleasure that night, climbing on to a train with Trev and George. We first visited the local burger house to line our stomachs, then climbed into a taxi and headed for the club. George and Trev were greeted with smiles and outstretched arms, giving the impression that an awful lot of their spare time had been spent there. Terry and I were introduced and made to feel very at home by Christian the owner and his team of barmaids.

Three hours of furious dancing took us through to midnight, with George looking slightly the worse for wear. As well as everything else, he was one of those infuriating swine who could actually dance, as opposed to just moving in a silly fashion. The time had come to relax in the club's back area. No dance floor or loud music, just comfy chairs and a bar, where the most commonly served beverage was coffee. Christian left the stand-in DJ to do his bit and came through to join us.

Being brought up in East Germany was obviously very different from Britain. We were made so welcome because we were Westerners. This was a country that was beginning to acquire everything that it had been deprived of for so long. They loved us and we treated them accordingly. The rest of that night and part of the morning was spent swapping stories with Christian and having a good laugh. All too soon, the time came to head off to the train station. The train journey was spent chatting to George who promised to talk to his landlord who had a spare room, so that we could move straight in on our return from Blighty. This would be a huge weight off our minds and allow us to enjoy our break that little bit more.

With just two days left, it was back to just keeping our heads down and getting on with the work, all the while hoping the time would go that little bit quicker. As usual, when you are wanting time to pass quickly, the days drag on for ever. A trip to the city centre was made to break up the day and with a purpose. Our last return trip to England had been that long coach journey. After sleeping in the train stations, earning very little money and finally burning down a perfectly adequate set of digs, the journey could have been made by bicycle and we would still have tried to enjoy every single mile of it. However, after returning to Leipzig by the same means, we had sworn to always fly in the future if we could afford to. The first travel agents that we saw on arriving in the city centre that day provided us with the tickets to carry out our promise to ourselves. Leipzig has its own airport, so convenience should have been the keyword. As we had found on more than one occasion, convenience was not a word that could be associated with our time in Germany, so this experience was bound to have a catch. Sure we had tickets, but not from Leipzig – from Berlin!

Yet another train journey didn't worry us unduly, as we were by that time well accustomed to the German railway system, having travelled through the whole country on day one and slept in two of their stations in various emergencies.

It was a shame that we were not able to fly from Leipzig, but this was soon forgotten when we realised that the Berlin flight enabled us to leave the very next day. All of a sudden the train journey didn't seem quite such a bind. As before, we would happily have used bikes to get to Berlin.

It is very strange how you never ever get remotely close to oversleeping on the morning that you are due to go home. True to form, we arrived at the station two hours early and waited for the first train to the capital. I had never visited Berlin, but along with the rest of the world I had sat watching the television pictures of the Wall finally coming down, seeing families reunited and seeing history being made. Now I was about to see it all first hand, taking it for granted that we would actually arrive.

For a change, the journey went smoothly without a single hitch. The train left on time and even arrived in Berlin five minutes early. The city's airport was approximately a twenty-five minute drive from the station. We could not risk catching a bus for fear of ending up back in Leipzig. It seemed so much easier just to leap in a taxi and scream, 'airport'. At least we were guaranteed to get where we wanted to be.

The next fifteen minutes were, without doubt, bizarre. The airport was on the opposite side of the city to the station and so the taxi took us straight through the middle of Berlin, warts and all. The area surrounding the train station was not unlike the part of Leipzig that we had been working in – building sites to the left and right, building sites in front and behind. Dotted amongst the cranes were rows of the very same living quarters that were such a familiar sight in Leipzig. They were huge buildings housing huge amounts of people. Advertising hoardings positioned everywhere carried posters persuading the natives to purchase things that I personally had never heard of, but were obviously very popular in the East at that time.

It wasn't too long before the Wall came into view. I say the 'Wall', yet the only way we could tell that was what it was, was that they had left the Brandenberg Gate standing, like one large, solid memorial to time gone by. I could still imagine those people charging through it when the good news broke. Without having even the tiniest amount of understanding of what it must have felt like, it was still a moving moment.

As well as a memorial to what had occurred, the Brandenberg Gate also served as a time machine. Within seconds of passing through it you had forgotten what the eastern side was like and instead looked in awe at the sights of the West. The old East was just that – old. The West was all gleaming office blocks, expensive houses, massive shopping complexes and advertising hoardings that displayed, in contrast to the East, products that were everyday items to me but were almost alien to the East only a year before. Maybe not alien, but certainly impossible to attain then. Before we had had time to take it all in, Berlin Airport loomed and our flight beckoned. We bade Berlin a fond farewell, raised our glasses to it in the departure lounge, then promptly forgot all about it as we boarded our flight for home.

Home was the same as ever; the same family and friends looking forward to seeing me and me being pleased that they did. Then there was Lucy, still not paid back fully. My reception from her was a long way off being perfect. I tried to understand how I would feel if it was her who owed me money, hoping things would eventually turn out all right. They would, but for all the wrong reasons.

That particular visit home was to take in Lucy's birthday. A day away shopping for the gift she wanted was my present to her. A very enjoyable day spent together with a smile on our faces was the prelude to a more satisfactory break than I had previously enjoyed and for a time things couldn't have been better, or so I thought. Reality would intrude from time to time with the thought that I would possibly have had just as much fun at home had I been away from Lucy completely and just spent my time at home relaxing from the twelve-hour days we had been working in Germany. In any case, I was pleased to be back.

As ever, when you are enjoying something, time passes at a startling rate. Time passed at home much quicker than the snail's pace in Germany and our week's break seemed to pass by in five minutes. However, it didn't seem quite such a wrench to leave that time, as the more time we were spending in Germany, the more comfortable it was beginning to feel. It had taken some time to lay down roots in Leipzig, but we had eventually achieved the feat. A whole new set of friends had been made, some of them of different nationalities and some of them just like us all, not there out of choice and just trying to make the most of it. Others had gone one step further than merely laying down roots and had a fully grown tree growing round them: their own flat, their own woman and a full wallet to add to their good fortune. It was summer and their tree was bearing ripe fruit. However, autumn is never far away and for some the leaves would fall a little harder than others.

Looking back, the only downside to working there was just that – we were working there. Other than that, we had slowly begun to realise that the experience wasn't all bad. Nobody would allow you to be miserable; there wasn't time. When work finished there was always something happening in a local bar to take your mind off everything, and sometimes due to the alcohol it was, quite literally, everything.

The usual round of fond farewells and kisses goodbye did not seem quite as bad, as our next tour of duty was to be the final one of '94. Seven weeks in Germany would take us up to Christmas followed by a six-week break to celebrate the festive season, a well-deserved break – for all but one. In retrospect, I wish the temptation to stay at home had got the better of me that time. If I could turn back the clock, I would have lost a few very good friends, but it would have been a small price to pay to blank out the events that would follow four weeks after our flight.

The return fight to Berlin was trouble free, with Terry and I exchanging our holiday stories. Our only concern was not being entirely sure whether we had anywhere to stay on our arrival in Leipzig. Our first task after touching down on German soil again was to head straight to the site, baggage and all, to find George who had promised before we left to talk to his landlord and make every effort to have a room waiting for us. If he had not been successful, it would be down to our powers of persuasion, a bit of grovelling and some hard cash in Trev's pocket to talk him into putting us up yet again. He had made it obvious to us before returning to England that we were beginning to cramp his pulling power and so it was an option we wanted to avoid. Still, pride vanishes very quickly when you are in trouble. Your friend can wait to get his leg over if it means you having somewhere to sleep.

We stepped on to the platform at Leipzig Station and straight into a taxi, pointing the driver in the direction of the site. Within a split-second of the taxi dropping us off George's familiar, over-cheerful voice could be heard and across he came in the manner we had become accustomed to, with the demeanour of a tremendously excited ten-year-old on Christmas morning. 'Hello, mate. Where the hell are we sleeping tonight?'

Fortunately for us, George had carried out his promise to have a chat with his landlord but true to form, he had left it until the very last minute, managing to get us into his own room but not until the next day.

The aforementioned grovelling and hard cash option proved to be a winner with Trev, who agreed to let us stay in his apartment one more night. Terry was knackered after the journey and made his way back to the flat as soon as Trev made the offer. George in his wisdom decided that a good night's sleep was not the remedy for my tiredness and instead insisted that he and I leap into his car and head off to Magdeburg to celebrate our return. We had arrived on a Saturday and with Sunday being our traditional recovery day, I agreed to his suggestion. Christian was informed of our impending arrival in a hastily made telephone call which was met with the offer of beds for the night at his house, enabling us to return the next day, hopefully refreshed.

The journey to Magdeburg on that evening could hardly be described as uneventful. George in his wisdom decided to ignore the route that he knew like the back of his hand and seek out a quicker alternative. It's never a good idea to start turning off familiar roads and veering into unknown territory at the best of times. You can then multiply the problems tenfold when you are in a foreign country in total darkness and you have recently filled the car's fuel tank with the wrong fuel.

There are two types of petrol in Germany, Verbleit and Super-Verbleit. We really should have foreseen that in the event of a fifty-fifty choice George was going to choose the wrong one. On that occasion he did not disappoint as I found out upon making our way along one of Germany's notoriously fast Autobahns at 30 m.p.h. with the vehicle jumping along like a kangaroo instead of rolling. Taking into account that we got lost on three occasions, the car's inability to move smoothly and the growing tension inside the vehicle, it could be described as nothing less than a miracle that we managed to arrive at Christian's club only two hours late! The knack of turning up everywhere late was yet another of George's fortes and so Christian and the rest of the gang didn't even bat an eyelid when we finally breezed in at two thirty in the morning.

When the prospect of living and working in Germany had first been discussed with Terry on the telephone, I hadn't been over eager. My impression of Germans before I had agreed to go over with Terry was that not one of them would have a sense of humour; they would all be brash, over-confident, selfish, aggressive and quite simply not much fun to be around. Some had fitted the bill perfectly but then so did some British people. We must have by coincidence found an area of the country where most of those traits were not particularly in evidence. Either that, or they were much the same as us after all and would not be attempting to bomb our houses the following week.

Christian was turning out to be the best possible example. He was always pleased to see us in his club and made absolutely sure that when he was in Leipzig he would visit us wherever we were working or living to say, 'Guten Tag!' and keep in touch. He was to do a little more than simply say, 'Guten Tag' in the future, extending the arm of friendship to realms that I wasn't even considering while I was attempting to dance or keeping him laughing in the coffee room. At the moment the extent of his friendship while we were visiting him in his club was to make concessions for us when the time came to pay our bill – at times a very large bill – by keeping it down to an absolute minimum for us. Good for his business? Maybe, but he was also becoming an extremely good mate as well. The sum total was that we had no desire at all to take our custom anywhere else.

After a drink and a quick look at a map to find where we had gone wrong on our travels, George's urge to dance eventually took a hold and that time became infectious as I decided to make a fool of myself an hour earlier than usual. My pathetic efforts soon came to a halt but it was obvious that George was in for a full hour, only returning to top up his fluid levels. I was finally joined in the coffee room by George who had left his customary puddle of sweat on the dance floor as a calling card. Any photographs of George taken during our trips to the club showed his body in a blur, looking as if he had just arrived out of a rainstorm. It was reminiscent of a dog shaking water off itself as only a dog could – or George could!

After a minute of wafting towels over sweaty heads, Christian ambled in to join us, leaving his partner in crime to take over the microphone for a short while. After ten minutes of cheerful banter I glanced over to my left and a shiver ran down my spine. A friend of Christian had arrived at the club, found nobody dancing and meandered through to see if there was anybody worth talking to in the resting area. There wasn't, but we were there, so that was her only choice. Christian greeted her and George was no stranger to her either as they had met on one of his previous trips, prior to me tagging along for the ride. She introduced herself to me as Romy and after regaining full use of my tongue I introduced myself to the gorgeous creature in front of me.

The mood in our camp became distinctly jovial as I moved into joke-telling mode. If one of George's fortes was dancing all night, one of mine is a memory for jokes. One reminds me of another and another, and so on, until I eventually run out of steam. Our German friends loved hearing our jokes and on a few occasions even managed to tell everyone the punch line, annoyingly before I reached it.

Romy's stamina was the first to fail as tiredness overtook her and she headed off for home, leaving me looking forward to the next time we met. Lucy? Lucy who? Just to make absolutely sure that my mind wouldn't be on my work for the next week, Romy promised as she left to meet us at the same time next weekend. Her departure made the three remaining coffee drinkers take a look at their watches. It was apparent that no beds would be seeing us that night as we were already well into the next day. The last coffee of the session was drunk and we finally left.

It was the first time in my life that I had left a nightclub at 10 a.m. It became apparent halfway through our return journey to Leipzig that we were not in the best of states for driving and so we decided to have a ten minute break to recharge the batteries, pulling over to the side of the road.

'Where the hell are we?' I remember hearing. A look at my watch and I saw that the time was 4 p.m.! We really should be heading back to the digs to collect Terry and all of our gear to take to our new home. The foot went on the gas once more.

At long last we arrived at the digs, tired and hungry, informing Terry of what had occurred the previous night. All of our baggage was placed into the car for the short journey to our new abode. Then it was unceremoniously dumped into one room and we concentrated on our choice of beds. With a total of two rooms to choose from, there wasn't an awful lot of choice when it came to deciding who slept where. Surprisingly, that dilemma was sorted out in approximately the same time as it took us to reach our tea hut at tea break on the site – about a minute. Terry grabbed a room all to himself and I duly spread my possessions around the second bed in George's room. It would be a pleasant change to share a room with somebody else after the weeks spent moving from room to room with Terry. I was lucky it was George who became my new room mate. We were both in Germany for the same reasons – mostly money orientated – we had a similar sense of humour and got on well together almost immediately. Eventually it becomes almost impossible to work and live together with a friend without becoming extremely pissed off with each other. The small habits that they have become harder to ignore until at last you need to get away. Circumstances had forced the change upon us and it came as a welcome relief.

The previous evening back at the club, George and myself had spoken about our respective jobs at length and the differences between the two. Terry and I were working for a price; the more work we did, the more money we earned. If we were prepared to work every hour of the day it could be a very lucrative system. However, the pitfalls are numerous – illness, weather, no supplies, the list goes on and we had encountered some of them on numerous occasions. We would often be standing around on the site waiting for supplies for hours and earning nothing when it was not even our fault. Sometimes we would feel ill and take a break – more money down the drain. We were rarely working in ideal circumstances and so it was not always possible to work productively.

In stark contrast to Terry and myself, George was working on the right site, in perfect circumstances. He, along with the rest of the masons (or plasterers, they could never decide which) was being paid on an hourly rate. Whenever they were on site they were paid, working or not. The desperation of the Germans to have the work finished quickly meant that they were highly unlikely to send anyone home early while it seemed that even the smallest amount of work could be finished. For that reason, it was that much easier to earn money by that system than by our own. If materials were in short supply it was the employer's fault and their employees would continue to be paid for simply being there until the foreman got fed up with waiting and cut his losses by calling it a day. This seems a much fairer method of earning your wages when driven almost entirely by greed with a small slice of idleness added to the equation. I had confirmed to George that I was indeed greed-orientated and was therefore desperate for him to find me a place with his firm in even the smallest capacity, expecting nothing to come from my pleas. My thinking was wrong, but my timing immaculate.

The work on the site that the plasterers had been brought in to do was coming to an end and rifts were beginning to appear between certain members of the team. George had become increasingly annoyed with his fellow workers and vice versa. He had, the day before our conversation, taken it upon himself to climb into his car and visit the neighbouring sites looking for potential vacancies. The other lads on the site had sarcastically wished him good luck and waved him off. I immediately agreed to finish my work on the site and go with him instead should he unearth any more work, thereby doubling my wages overnight. His initial attempts had proved fruitless and he was going for one last look the following day. I wished George good luck and crossed my fingers hoping that something, anything could be found.

On arriving back at the digs that night my fingers uncrossed as George informed me that he had found a job and we would be starting on the following Monday. However, he had dug himself a small hole by making a promise to the foreman that his team would comprise four men and unless things changed dramatically, so far there were only the two of us.

A trip back to the site that we had just left was the order of the day. All of George's workmates who had mocked him when hearing of his attempts to find pastures new, looked more than a little startled when learning of his success. Despite the fact that their work was nearly done, they all chose to ignore George's offer of a job, deciding instead in a very British kind of way to stick with what they knew in the hope of something coming up when their present work finished. There then followed an hour of listening to ten men trying to tell us that it would never last, that we were fools, etc., and in the end laughing at all of them, leaving the site without so much as a goodbye. It is interesting to discover what people are really like when you better yourself and they can't even be bothered to try.

*

It was Thursday. We would be starting our job in four days and had promised that we would arrive, four men together, eager to work. It didn't take a Mensa-approved IQ to see that there were only two of us. We decided that it would be virtually impossible to do enough to pass ourselves off as two men, let alone four! Two more eager beavers had to be found and fast. Terry needed some convincing about the merits of quitting the job that we had made our own but soon saw sense when the potential earnings figures were placed in front of him. One down, one to go.

There was absolutely nobody in the city whom Terry and I had met who had been likeable enough to offer the job to and George's entourage had made their feelings towards him very clear, with most of the words used being of the four-letter variety. Only one method remained and so the address book that George carried with him everywhere was surgically removed from his pocket and a process of elimination began. After examining the pros and cons of each individual, one name eventually presented itself that needed no discussion.

Glyn was not new to any of us. He had been working with George on the site a month previously, an easygoing kind of guy and liked by all. He was in exactly the same boat as everyone else – broke and needing money badly. He had succeeded in his quest on his first visit. On leaving for home, his finances looked healthy. A week after his return, all of the debts that led him to Germany in the first place were paid up and he was back to square one again, broke. The only problem he had had on his first visit was that he had found it much more difficult to settle than the rest of us. He had been forced to stay working for longer than he had anticipated just to pay the telephone bills that he and his wife had run up in both countries, the result of making calls lasting more than ninety minutes every day of his stay. On the day that he left for home, we had thrown a large party for him, partly for him to celebrate the end of his trip and partly for everyone else to celebrate the fact that we would no longer have to endure his day-long bouts of moaning and generally feeling sorry for himself, while we were quietly taking bets on how long it would be before we all saw him again. The bets, the ribbing and the laughter at his expense had to be done at a distance. He was a large muscular man with a liking for one too many bottles of beer – not the best combination, yet more humorous when he again fell into a depression.

The mobile phone that George carried with him for no other reason than trying to look good appeared, and Glyn was duly called. He was still broke and his job prospects at home were not looking any better than they had when he had been forced to leave the first time around. After his initial refusal of our offer, some gentle persuasion resulted in him agreeing to discuss the chance with his wife and call back later. His decision was just as important to the three of us sat waiting in Germany. If our team could not be expanded, then none of us would be working and with

Christmas just around the corner, that would have been a disaster. It was hard enough to handle returning home with a quarter of what was expected, but returning home to a miserable Christmas, totally present-free would be far too shameful to contemplate and so we sat with bated breath awaiting Glyn's call.

By the stroke of midnight the mobile phone had been silent for four hours and our preparation for a return home with heads bowed were being made. Then as nooses were being tightened around light fittings the phone finally rang and George covered the length of our room at the speed of light to get to it before it stopped. Not much chance of that as George greeted Glyn before the phone's second ring had ceased. Glyn had decided to put himself through one last tour until Christmas and so our team was set. Much celebrating delayed any thoughts of sleep, finally succumbing to rest our bodies before the final working day on the site we knew so well and informing the Germans of our intention to quit.

It was a sad moment when our work was done and it came to leaving the site. The majority of the German workforce seemed genuinely sorry to see us go, seeing us off in their own inimitable style, crushing our hands with their vice-like handshakes.

We walked over the entire site as we made our final calculations to present to the company in order to receive our final pay-out, adding an occasional fabrication to boost the result! We were leaving so there was nothing to lose. Thomas, the foreman, was the last man to see us off, giving yet another crippling handshake to each of us before bidding us Auf Wiedersehen. This would be our last visit to that area and so a final coffee at Seaweed's café was most definitely called for. With some difficulty, our reasons for leaving were explained and the farewell was a tearful one from the woman herself as we departed for pastures new.

With only the weekend separating us from the real work, we were utterly determined that it was to be enjoyed. Then the problem of accommodation sprang to mind. Our new place of work was some distance away and a hotel nearer was preferable. Terry stayed behind to round up our tools, etc., while George and myself set off in the direction of the site, keeping our eyes alert for any potential digs that we might come across. At first, looking is all you can do, as you drive around trying to find somewhere suitable.

The 'Irish Haus' was a name given to us on being turned away from our first enquiry about digs. Leipzig, like the rest of Europe, has an array of cultures tucked away within its boundaries and it is riddled with Irish establishments to cater for the potentially huge alcoholic consumption levels of the four Irishman who live in the city and the rest of the nationalities who seem to believe that Ireland is only memorable for drinking itself into a stupor at every available opportunity. We had already undergone the Leipzig builders' initiation ceremony of visiting as many of the places as is humanly possible in a weekend until eventually double vision almost convinces you that some of the bars had been visited before. Having a forty-eight hour party is fun once but the demands of work made everyone less than eager for a second. For that reason we chose to ignore the tip and continue our search for a more peaceful environment in which to stay.

After two more refusals including another mention of the Irish Haus we were left with little choice but to hunt down the obviously legendary hotel/public house. It was either that or staying at a hotel just far enough away to make travelling to and from the site add another hour or two on to an already long day. After a lengthy search of the area involving stopping bemused Germans, asking them for directions and driving away after understanding not one word of their replies, the Irish Haus finally appeared in front of us more by luck than judgement.

Four grubby Englishmen covered in dust and cement were leaving the premises as we entered, leading us to believe that this was indeed the right place. The bar was virtually deserted but a cheerful barmaid complete with broad Irish accent greeted us as we sat down to order a coffee. The look on her face told us that she was not often asked to put the kettle on behind the bar and with a chuckle our orders were relayed to the one other member of staff on duty in the kitchen. With her very best saleswoman voice the barmaid promptly described the hotel's Full English Breakfast – eggs, bacon, fried bread, sausages etc. and our drools said it all. Ten minutes later paradise on a plate arrived in front of two disbelieving newcomers. We were going to like this place. No – we were going to love it!

One room containing four beds was vacant, but not for long. Our deposits were paid and our lodgings had been found. Terry's and our belongings were duly brought back to our new abode and Terry was left to sample the atmosphere of the place while George and myself made the now obligatory trip to Christian's club after attempting to smarten ourselves up. After all, it was Saturday night and it was good now and then to not look like you had just climbed out of a rubbish dump. A new job was starting on the Monday morning and another night of dreadful dancing, joke-telling and a few drinks was necessary to charge our batteries prior to another session of trying to impress German employers and fellow employees. Not an easy task. The fact that you are an outsider in any country always puts you a rung further down the ladder of acceptance within any circle of people, either socially or at work.

The journey to see Christian was preceded by a further round of telephone calls to pass on my new address. The small matter of my birthday was looming on the not too distant horizon and it would be a pleasant change to receive some mail from home in celebration of the said event and to escape from the same old people and routines for a while. The calls home were to be my last contact with friends and relatives for a much longer time than I was anticipating.

'I will see you in three weeks,' was my parting shot to anyone I spoke to and to a certain extent it was very true, at least for them. It would be twice as long before I knew that anyone from back home in England was around me in any shape or form.

Perhaps it was a good thing or maybe it was coincidence that for the first time in a while Lucy seemed pleased to hear from me. The cheerfulness on the other end of the line turned to ecstasy when I explained that my movement into a fresh working environment would enable my finances to extend to paying back all of the money that Lucy had quite rightly been expecting ever since my arrival in Leipzig, now some six months ago. The conversation momentarily turned to talk of how much we both were looking forward to my impending arrival back at home for Christmas. There was only three weeks left to see through, before I boarded the plane and forgot about work for a month. Our tickets had been booked and paid for some weeks previously. Terry, George and myself, along with three of the lads back on the site that we had just left, had all booked our seats together and had, in effect, reserved one tiny section of the aircraft in which to have our own private Christmas party and no doubt annoy the hell out of every other passenger who had been unfortunate enough to find themselves on the same plane. Luckily for the passengers, they were to be spared that ordeal.

In the meantime, I said my goodbyes to Lucy and put down the phone before joining George in the car for the journey to Magdeburg. The radio was immediately cranked up to full blast in preparation for the night's enjoyment; our ears needed to be accustomed to loud music before entering the club. It was a very enclosed establishment due to the fact that it was an old bunker used by the Stasi police back in the East's darker times. Prolonged exposure to loud music in that environment almost led to deafness to more than one partygoer. The coffee room was an escape from the noise, used at some point by everyone in the bunker. As for myself, it was totally the opposite. I would sit in the coffee room all night and only venture into the noise for as long as it takes a kettle to boil. You can only take being laughed at for so long!

Pulling into the car park I noticed that there was still an hour to go until midnight and that night was going to be one hell of a long haul in the coffee room, perhaps leading to severe caffeine addiction in those of us without the ability to pass off even a resemblance of being a dancer.

Christian's infectious smile greeted us once again on entering the club. He was doing his usual sterling work behind the microphone and turntables, however on this occasion being joined by two Englishmen, one of whom was convinced that he could do a better job of livening up the proceedings. Surprise, surprise, he could and so George the DJ was born, needing a heavy-duty wrench to prise him away from being the centre of attention, a position he craved ninety per cent of every day! I assumed my role as his straight man, standing for thirty minutes passing the man records as he whipped up a previously staid atmosphere into one of fun, tinged with more than a touch of bemusement as the energetic Englishman continued to talk absolute rubbish in a variety of stupid voices. That at least was my reaction – and I understood the language! Christ only knows what the Germans thought he was saying, but it worked.

As well as making the Germans get up and dance, George was also stoking up his own passion for exercise and after bowing to the audience, his natural instincts finally took over with him handing the microphone back to a well-rested Christian and going for it big time on the dance floor, until he dropped. I fought and fought, but could not stave off my own desire to spend three minutes making a fool of myself in a seventies disco-dancing kind of way and then getting the hell out of there.

The coffee lounge was quiet, so I took my place and relaxed at a safe distance from the speakers. Romy entered the club and came across to join me, much to my surprise. I was now beginning to feel slightly guilty as thoughts of Lucy back home came into my mind. Make no mistake, even the smallest glimmer of hope from Romy's direction and I would have happily – what is that saying about hindsight again?

Romy's English was superb. Within a minute or two you forgot she was German and felt like you had known her all your life. On that particular occasion, the conversation was to revolve around her desire to study at a university in England. Quite why she chose to discuss the topic with me, I will never know. I was stuck working a thousand miles away from home, something that I had had no desire to do at all. Had I had any experience of university life, there would have been little chance of me being sat with her in the first place. Not being even remotely scholarly, there was not a chance of me ever knowing enough about the lifestyle and consequently there was never going to be a great deal that I could say that would be of any use to her, but I tried anyway in a pathetic attempt to keep her sitting with me.

As the minutes ticked by, Christian and George joined the potential student and her trying companion to end the night with the usual copious amounts of coffee followed by a similar volume of jokes, culminating in sheer exhaustion.

The three *amigos* parted company with Romy and headed back to Christian's home for a couple of hours' rest before journeying back to Leipzig. Christian would be taking the ride with us as a cheap method of returning to his flat in the city, a flat that would prove to be a Godsend in the coming weeks.

After parting company with Christian, we headed back to team up with Terry again and squeeze all our possessions which we had emptied out of the digs into the car, before going to the Irish Haus. The amount of practice we had all had at hurriedly switching allegiance from one landlord to another had made us experts at the game. The Irish Haus was to be our seventh place to lay our heads in a mere six months.

The place was busier than it had been when George and myself had wandered in unsure of what to expect and desperate for food and a bed each. After all our previous experiences such as sleeping in train stations, backs of vans and crummy digs, this was in a different league. There were genuinely friendly staff, hearty greetings, firm handshakes and drinks bought for us by some of the other occupants. It was our own little piece of Britain tucked away in the middle of East Germany.

Coming into a place packed with people who are pleased to see you, talk your language and are in exactly the same boat as you makes a welcome break from having to look for potential work, potential living quarters and potential friends while trying to earn a living on the site. It would be good to escape from the people who we were already spending twelve hours a day working with to spend the rest of our waking hours with new faces.

However, top of the list of reasons for choosing the place was the chance to eat proper meals rather than spending the days snacking on chocolate bars and cold or uncooked meat. We had yet to sample the goods, but hoped that the food would be good after the breakfast on the day we found the place. Our meals arrived and we were not disappointed. The three courses served were devoured in no time.

The stay at the bar that night lasted longer than usual, until the early hours in fact. The main topic of conversation centred around the lies that we would have to have rehearsed when asked by our new foreman where the promised fourth member of the team was. Much discussion and deep thought ended with concocting a story that was far too devious for even the most suspicious foreman to disbelieve. Glyn's failure to arrive until our second day on the site would be explained by the statement, 'He's missed his flight.' Genius! Surely they had never heard that one before!

The short drive to our new place of work soon turned into a very long drive indeed. We had failed to pay attention to the positioning of the site in relation to the hotel and consequently became very lost, at one point thinking ourselves back at the site we had left behind. Eventually though we drove on to the site with our heads down, an hour late. We hadn't needed to feel embarrassed, as the foreman greeted us like old friends and turned a disinterested, deaf ear to our lies surrounding Glyn's arrival. It was most important for him to have any number of workers available. Speed was the priority and Glyn's expected arrival the following day appeared to be a bonus in his eyes.

The rest of that day was to be spent doing nothing else but walking around the site looking at what had to be done and introducing ourselves to other Brits who were already recruited and were familiar faces to the Germans running the job. It was always necessary when starting new employment to talk to the experienced people who knew what to do and where to go and what not to do to avoid upsetting the short-tempered nationals. We were to receive no help at all from our fellow English-speaking co-workers; they had only been on the site a week longer than ourselves. The number of Brits who had little knowledge of their employers had just doubled in the space of a morning! Luckily, 'B' team as we tagged them were just as pleased as us to see some friendly Brits and the work took on a slightly less bleak appearance. A few new personalities to share a laugh with was never going to be a bad thing.

We did not need telling what we would be working on; they were clearly visible. We were to work on what was to be the first expensive housing estate that we were aware of in Leipzig. It was clear that the old apartment blocks would eventually disappear and be replaced by Western luxury. This particular estate consisted of approximately twenty houses that would sell for an estimated £200,000 each. Team A and Team B's jobs were to plaster the exterior of each and every one of them. The houses were superb, but unfortunately the rest of the site was an utter disgrace. The word 'quagmire' was a perfect description. There was a dirt track that led through the centre of the site that enabled us to reach all of the houses. By the time we arrived at the site it was winter and the adverse weather conditions normally associated with that season, combined with the multitude of heavy vehicles passing through, had cut the track up so badly that safety boots had to be worn at all times, not for safety but to keep your feet dry in the intense cold.

When you spend your working days on a building site, you find that it isn't often that you come into contact with a hygienic toilet, and this site was no exception. Dotted around the area at regular intervals were those horrible plastic cubicles that make no attempt to disguise what they actually are. Following the trend and taking the fashion one step further, ours were lurid luminous pink and ten of the newly christened 'Turdises' lit up the site nicely. Was the bright colouring to enable us to find the bloody things? No!

Not one of them had been emptied for quite some time and so the smell emanating from each of them was enough to alert us to their whereabouts and duly avoid them if at all possible! In fact, they blended in nicely with the rest of the site. It too was wet, foul-smelling, muddy and all in all a very depressing place to be. We needed to work to take our minds off the rest of the place.

Our first task was to be our own team's first stab at 'machine plastering'. This was a simple procedure involving the machine doing the mixing for you and then feeding huge quantities of the mix through a pipe and pumping it on to the walls at speed. Terry would be loading the machine until Glyn's arrival, George would be doing the necessary finish on the walls and I would be standing grasping the end of the nozzle and directing the mixture on to the walls. We prepared ourselves for our first attempt, the one that would impress our new employers and prove to them that we were the best team in the whole of Germany. Terry loaded the machine and stood for a moment staring at the big red button. With some trepidation Terry eventually took the bull by the horns and stabbed the button. We waited. I stood atop the first level of scaffolding surrounding the house, looking for all the world like I was preparing myself to extinguish an inferno. I knew what to do, I had seen *The Towering Inferno*. I gripped the hose as tightly as I possibly could and waited with bated breath for the first immensely powerful surge of the plaster mix. The hose began to vibrate gently in my hands, the vibrations turned into rumbles and so I began to grip even more tightly. This was it, the hose was throbbing violently in my hands, the recoil was surely going to throw me a full ten feet backwards off the scaffolding! I placed my feet into the best possible position to counteract the force I would soon be experiencing. I closed my eyes and gritted my teeth, to block the pain I would surely experience on landing ten feet below. The hose shook for one last time – my bowels shook for the first time. The surge swelled through the pipe and then it happened – a blob of plaster the size and shape of a hamster plopped harmlessly on to the toe of my left boot. As an encore to that less than impressive display, the machinery itself made a loud bang and shuddered to a halt and all attempts to revive it failed. The foreman in his excitement had not realised that this machine seemed to date back to before the wall even went up! On the plus side, we were still getting paid. We were promised that the machine would be fixed and up and running in time for our arrival the following morning. Day one over. Glyn hadn't missed much.

We soon decided that a full day's pay could still be gleaned from the machine debacle and so off we went to the other side of the site to talk to Team B trying all the time to appear to be working, should any of the foreman's lackeys arrive to check what was happening. It never occurred to us to ask, but we could never work out how Team B became a team. They were, after all, two cockneys and two Welshmen. They could only have met in Germany or they would have had to have done a tremendous amount of commuting to work together back at home. To be brutally honest, we didn't really care, so long as they didn't get in our way. They seemed to feel the same way about us and the mutual understanding stood us in good stead.

When you are working together with complete strangers in a foreign land, at some point the conversation will turn to where you are living and where you go for a drink. It transpired that Team B were staying in the hotel right next door to the one that Terry and myself had left without paying our bills way back on tour number one. It was apparently very sparse, only having facilities for guests who were merely passing through and not actually living there for any length of time. We took great delight as we began to describe the luxuries available to us in our lovely abode. Four pairs of eyes lit up and four mouths drooled on hearing of the food we had eaten since we had moved there. Various comments were spoken on more than one occasion, words like 'heaven', 'perfect' and 'jammy bastards' among them. George and Terry prolonged the agony by claiming to have acquired the last room in the place. Then Chris, Team B's leader, mentioned the large van that ferried all of them and their tools to work with room for – oh, let's see – four more! This put a whole new complexion on the situation. With Glyn arriving next day, we would no longer have room in George's car to travel to and from work. There was barely room for two, due to George's liking of small cars, in which practicality was a distant second place to aesthetics. We would lose valuable time making two trips to the site simply to get four people working. A new mode of transport was urgently required.

'Why don't you come and stay at our place?' was an invitation they accepted gladly and so promises were made about enquiring at the Irish Haus about vacancies that night after our meal had been devoured.

As we entered the place after work that day it was like walking into the local pub on the corner of your street. The staff were on first-name terms with us already. The enquiries were made and a room for Chris and the boys was set aside for them to move into the next day. It would be a busy day as the final piece in our own jigsaw, namely Glyn, would be arriving at an unknown time. We couldn't be absolutely positive when, or if, he would show. His ability to feel homesick as soon as his feet left his own doorstep would probably get the better of him this time. However, no matter what happened during the day, I would be doing my very best to enjoy myself. I had never dreamed that I would one day be celebrating my birthday in Germany of all places, but that year, like it or loathe it, I would. The ritual piss-up was due to start the moment work finished and George and I had been invited over to Magdeburg for the weekend to spend our time flitting between the homes of Christian and Romy.

December 3rd 1994 was the most cheerful morning I had spent in Germany in all the time we had been there. Birthday cards had arrived from Lucy and anyone else who had managed to find out my address. My arrival in the bar for breakfast was announced by a very loud and equally sarcastic version of 'Happy Birthday' being sung. I was sorely tempted to have a rest on my day of celebration, pack work in for the day and just lounge around the bar enjoying myself in a warm room instead of working on a freezing building site. George quite literally dragged the temptation out of me as he pulled me through the door, claiming that if he was going everyone was going. I would no doubt have been just as selfish had the tables been turned.

A fixed machine in perfect working order was unveiled at the site on our arrival. A list of jobs was then handed to us that was long enough to keep us employed in the country until well into the next millennium. With that much work to do, we had no doubt in our minds that we were earning every penny. Of course, we would all have unexplained disappearances from time to time, but what the hell – the rest of the time, our friendly German fore-man/sergeant major made sure that we were not slacking. At least this meant we were so busy that the day would no longer drag along with all of us counting the minutes.

In no time at all, the eight of us were happily clambering into the back of Chris's van and heading off to our digs where the new boys would sample the atmosphere of the place for the very first time, while we waited for Glyn to arrive and complete Team A. The first hot meal that our new mates had eaten for a week was consumed as they continually thanked us for pointing them in the direction of their new digs. As the beer was starting to flow freely, the door opened and in walked Glyn, looking decidedly more cheerful than the rest of his team had expected. However, it was still only his first day away from home and his yearning for the place had yet to establish itself fully. A meal, a bottle of beer and a laugh with old mates postponed the inevitable homesickness, for the first day at least.

All too soon, nine of us were once again climbing into the back of the van with slightly less urgency than we always managed on leaving the site. On our ever-depressing arrival on the site, the foreman quickly pointed us to the house on which we were to be working that day. The first task on a new house was always to hunt out a cubby hole where we could all take turns disappearing for a skive throughout the day – hey, we're only human!

There was still a lot of internal work to be done in the house, a fact that became obvious immediately upon entry.

Ten feet inside the entrance to the house on the ground floor was a stairwell, just that, a stairwell, no stairs and more importantly, no safety barriers surrounding it. Coming from the area of Europe that we all hailed from, this was a puzzle. Ground floor... awaiting stairs to go down... no never seen that before. Another introduction into the German way of life. Most of the men, no, all of the men standing around the stairwell assumed that it would simply be a room that was an ideal place in which to store all of those unwanted items that every home gathers, in short, a dumping ground.

The foreman on the site took a break from his duties and explained that most Germans have a cellar and not to use as we had all thought. These cellars were important rooms in which friends would gather to socialise, obviously meaning drink and drink some more. Maybe our foreman was stretching the truth. I will never know, as my only visit to the cellar in the coming weeks was not destined to be a happy one.

'Welcome to work, Glyn!' was followed by the prophetic reply, 'Jesus Christ! Some poor bastard is going to go head first down that one day!'

No, somebody would surely see the danger and do something quickly, after all we were dealing with the efficient Germans. Ignorance was not bliss for a change; it was potentially lethal. The danger on the sites was often overlooked. Most of the time our heads were filled with thoughts of where we were going to sleep that night or whether we would ever get paid for the long hours we had put in. More importantly, just like the rest of the population, we all went through the days knowing that 'it will never happen to me'.

Unfortunately, it has to happen to someone and so it simply doesn't work like that. If only it was a perfect world! If it was we would all live our lives almost worry-free, relaxed and, above all, safe.

As we stood around the stairwell, safe in the knowledge that nobody in our little group was going to come to any immediate harm, all of the jokes about backflips, somersaults and perfect tens were cheerfully thrown around, along with more than one mention of Greg Louganis, the unfortunate American diver who had smashed his head on the way down from a diving board of similar height to the platform on which we were all standing. Whenever the incident was mentioned we would all wince in unison and comment on the severe headaches that the poor chap must have suffered from in the days following the accident, as well as the ones that he must still have whenever he thought back and remembered the pain of crashing into the board. After we had used up our sick senses of humour we took one last look at the stairwell and walked off, instantly forgetting all about the potential danger and moving on to the next prospective skiving area, still chuckling about the unfortunate accident that Mr Louganis had suffered only a moment before plunging into that swimming pool.

The search of the house came to an end after we had paired off to save time, resulting in Glyn and I discovering the perfect place to hide in for a few moments and so we immediately took full advantage. The next thirty minutes was spent doing nothing more stressful than quizzing each other on our knowledge of football.

After a morning of 'hard' work we all retired to the tea hut designated for the British workers and took an hour's break with the subject of my birthday entering the conversation on more than one occasion. Celebrating your birthday is quite strange when you are sat around the table with a group of people, and then for no reason at all you stop to look around and realise that everyone around you was a stranger six months beforehand. Your family, girlfriend and all of your friends are in another country. It is then that despite the laughter around you, you can still feel very alone. As our break was coming to an end, George's precious mobile phone began to ring. George quickly answered and found that it was Christian calling to inform us that our weekend with Romy had been postponed for another week. I began to feel extremely sorry for myself and decided to call Lucy back at home, so made my way to the nearest telephone. The conversation with Lucy was a touch forced from her end of the line but then I delivered the *coup de grâce*. All of my outstanding debts to her would be repaid by the end of that week. I was wished happy birthday and told how much I was loved. I didn't see through it and felt quite happy. This new-found cheer pushed me into telephoning everyone I knew who possessed a telephone for a brief conversation with each of them. Unknown to me, it was to be the last real conversation I was to have with any of them for two months.

A quiet weekend passed without incident. The Irish Haus was beginning to feel like home. It was the first whole weekend George and myself had spent there since we had moved in and the good rest and money saved would enable us to enjoy ourselves that little bit more the following weekend. We now had only two weeks to go until we boarded the flight home for four long weeks of Christmas holiday. It was a pleasant thought. We were even looking forward to the flight and seeing our old friends from the first site who had booked the seats with us. All of us for a change would have a lot of money in our pockets to take home and nothing could stop us enjoying the month,

The penultimate week on site started with the first snow we had seen in the country. When it's freezing cold all day it isn't only harder to work, it is simply too hard to build up the enthusiasm for the job and keep it. When we had first arrived on the site it was difficult enough working in a swamp. Now that the swamp was frozen solid it was as near to impossible as you could get. A rise in the temperature was to be no help, as when the snow and ice melted the ground and scaffolding upon it became incredibly treacherous. It seems ironic now, but we all felt nervous and at risk outside and safe inside one of the houses.

We all spent the day creeping around the scaffolding, watching every step in order to keep our balance. The Germans on the site were becoming increasingly irritated as we took every available opportunity to sod off into the warmth for ten minutes on a rotation system, ensuring that only one of us wasn't working at any one time. Glyn and myself mastered the system very early as our current job was plastering the wall on one end of the house up at its highest point, where the scaffolding didn't quite reach. In order to do the job, we had no choice but to construct some makeshift scaffolding which was made by resting planks of wood from the scaffolding to a stanchion supporting the apex. Below this unsteady construction was the ground, about thirty feet down and above it we stood a ladder to reach the very tip of the wall. Thinking nothing of kicking the ice off our boots and climbing on this contraption, the wall got finished. Sometimes you had to risk your neck to get the work done and get paid. The ladder went back in that stairwell where it had come from and it was time for the next challenge.

Friday came and a week of slipping and sliding and dangerous jobs was at last coming to an end. George and myself conserved our energy to be fit for Christian's club the next day. Romy had called to say she wouldn't even be in the country this time, as she was off skiing. I took that as a brush-off, but we decided to go and have a good time anyway. Friday night was spent exchanging large sums of money with each other over a few beers and a game of poker.

Getting out of bed every morning at 5 a.m. was an ordeal, especially in the current sub-zero temperatures. Saturday morning was no different, although a tiny chink of light was provided by Chris, who had nicked a football off the Germans the day before, so our skives would at least be very immature and enjoyable.

The working day started with all of us dodging the dangerous work, leaving it to the small number of Germans who were on site to work instead of just ordering the Brits about. Unusually we had an easy day, just finishing off work that had already been started. That was what the foreman asked us to do, but in reality the day turned into one long game of football with a few work breaks. I couldn't wait to get home for Christmas but was now enjoying being there almost totally. When Terry and I first arrived we had nothing at all, no money, friends, digs or indeed any form of social life. Now, the opposite applied. The fact that we all got on so very well was the most important aspect. Any problems that one of us had were soon forgotten as the remaining lads were certainly not going to be dragged down by having any miserable sods associating with them. Glyn, pretending to be Geoff Hurst, banged in the last goal of the day and reminded the Germans of 1966, who in turn reminded us of every year since. Chris pulled up in the van, we all piled in and prepared ourselves for the weekend. Within an hour of returning to the Irish Haus, George and myself, or the 'Magdeburg Two' as we were now known, had bathed, shaved, dressed and set off for Christian's.

The week's break had left George suffering from serious withdrawal symptoms and desperately needing to dance to shake them off. We made it in record time and were greeted on the door by Christian's brother, Sebastian or just plain Basti, as everyone called him. Drinks were bought and after sitting down for a full minute, George was up and on the dance floor. My four minutes of stupidity ended in the usual fashion, when people began to point and laugh in my direction. George, as ever, did more work in the following ten minutes than he had done all the previous week.

It soon became time to settle round our usual table in the coffee room. This week, our gathering had spread across to the next table as well, with Basti joining us and the two barmaids as it wasn't that busy. Christian's insatiable appetite for jokes managed to stem itself for at least ten minutes, until he could no longer resist. He gave me the nod and the onslaught began. On that occasion, bets had been taken on how long I would keep going. The length of time wasn't so impressive when we took into account the amount of time spent repeating punchlines and explaining them over and over again, very slowly to overcome the difficulties in translation. On more than one occasion an entire night of explaining a joke would fail to bring even the hint of a smile to perplexed German faces. No matter; you still could not wish for a better audience.

All the bets that had been taken that evening were held over until the following weekend, as for no apparent reason I felt an irresistible urge to hit the dance floor and make a fool of myself for the second time. Once in a night was foolish and two was verging on suicidal. For a full half-hour, *Saturday Night Fever* came to Magdeburg in the form of a skinny white Englishman who had just crossed the thin line between being cheerfully friendly and just plain drunk. *Saturday Night Fever* to me and simply 'Fever' to any of the onlookers!

As I fell into my usual chair in the coffee room, after my truly pathetic attempts to take the role of club dancer from George, I laughed to myself. George had had a similar urge to myself and stepped into my shoes and was keeping the troops entertained with his repertoire of two jokes. I listened to his number one joke for the seventh time and realised how I was thoroughly enjoying myself, as was everyone around me.

I could not work out why I was always so reluctant to return to Germany whenever I went home to England but in truth, it was simple: the part of the week that everyone enjoyed lasted for about three hours and none of those moments stick in your memory long enough to erase the other six days and twenty-one hours. Consequently, by the time you got back to normality at home, you didn't have long enough to forget that you were returning to what was ninety per cent cold, wet, building sites and concern at the ever-present threat that you were not going to get paid as your employers disappeared into the night.

Another enjoyable time soon passed. George's final joke failed to raise even a glimmer of a smile and I was too exhausted to do anything other than return to Christian's and get a well-earned four hours of sleep.

Christian's ever-cheerful face peered into our room to wake us from our blissful slumber. George managed to rise, dress and vanish on one of his numerous female conquests before breakfast was served. I was about to take Christian through another free English lesson by helping him to understand a rented video with no subtitles. I was saved from that dubious pleasure as the doorbell rang.

The two barmaids from the nightclub had been bored enough to visit and drag us off to somewhere interesting. Their idea of interesting was my idea of a normal Friday night out back at home. We all climbed into a hairdryer on wheels (or to give it its proper name, a Trabant) and headed off towards the local English pub. In Germany, two snooker tables and a video game seem to be the standard requirement in an establishment and then it can be thought of as an English pub. Your average German can certainly wield a cue and play a mean game of pool but if you double the size of the table and call the game snooker you instantly become unbeatable and therefore appear to be very good indeed. What promised to be a dull two hours turned into an uplifting experience for me but pure tedium for my friends.

I accepted apologies all round for their inability to play the game and promised to give them some lessons the following weekend. Christian made his way home, as with immaculate timing George returned from his liaison and we set off for Leipzig once more, finally arriving back on the stroke of midnight. It had been a fine weekend. I had not seen Romy but hell, I'd be back all the following year anyway and would have plenty of time to return and see our newly-made friends. Once again, ignorance was bliss.

The usual stressful atmosphere greeted the alarm clock on Monday morning, a fact made more apparent to me as the bleeping timepiece hurtled past my ear and turned itself off at speed against a wall. The usual extravagant weekday breakfast of coffee and toast was devoured and we all braved the winter air to make our way to another day of toil. On arrival, the normal ten-minute skive took place in our tea hut and ended as we all paired off, moving with well-rehearsed speed in order to try and be first to the better jobs that remained. The only criteria that a job had to have to be in this category was that it had to be away from prying eyes, the foreman's, for example. Having a German nearby constantly pushing for the work to be done almost before you had started it, didn't make for the most comfortable atmosphere to be working in. The work was hard enough to enjoy without being pressured twelve hours a day. On that morning I teamed up with Glyn in the chase for a plum job. Unfortunately, all the best ones went and after a few minutes of desperate searching, we ended up with the last available job on the site and probably the most precarious in the whole of Germany.

Most of the lads on the site had been forced into qualifying for and receiving the diplomas for the much maligned, mostly unheard of trade of 'rickety death-traps construction'. It certainly is not something that you are ever taught, yet if you wanted to work successfully in Germany at that time, it was necessary to become a dab hand immediately. Glyn and I had been awarded distinctions for the example that we knocked up that morning. In order to reach the apex of one side of an unfinished house, you simply climb up the scaffolding, finish the job and move on – on a building site in most other countries that is, but not in the former East Germany. It was plain to see that things worked slightly differently here. None of the mercenaries on the site could work out whether our German friends were having some form of sick joke at our expense by erecting all of the scaffolding approximately three feet short of the top of the buildings. This was where our death-trap construction became an essential part of the job. We were constantly being pressed by the men in charge to finish the work, yet often we would find insufficient preparations had been made for the job to be completed safely.

Glyn and myself tried every possible combination of death-trap that it was possible to construct with the materials nearby, finding each one unable to reach the top despite various uncomfortable, sometimes amusing, bodily contortions. With Christmas only two weeks away, our wages were top of the priority list and so a brain-racking session was the order of the day, to think of a way to successfully finish the work. A miniature skive began and after a couple of cigarettes and approximately forty football trivia questions, it dawned on us that our brain-racking session had turned into a full-blown skive. I realised this when, instead of discussing how the next phase of the job was to be concluded, I was muttering, 'Leeds United,' in response to another football trivia question.

After five minutes of desperately trying to outwit each other to no avail, we finally returned to the subject of our rickety scaffolding. The short break had clearly done us some good as we soon hit upon the wonderful idea of finding a ladder and balancing it precariously on top of what had already been constructed. After trying very hard to think of a better alternative that might well have been marginally safer, the conclusion was reached that if we were to escape the wrath of the impatient German foreman, we had no choice other than sticking with this bright idea. The solution was agreed upon and now the only problem was finding a ladder. This surely wouldn't be too difficult as we were on a building site, for God's sake!

However, we soon realised the only ladder that we could remember seeing during our time on the site was the one that we had all observed perched up against the stairwell that had looked so dangerous to us only days before. I am not sure if it was Glyn or myself who had the idea of using that particular ladder, as from that moment on my memory of the events that followed becomes a little unclear, for reasons about to become painfully obvious. I was either chosen or I volunteered to fetch the said ladder and off I trotted to fetch the final unsteady piece of our Grade One standard rickety death-trap jigsaw! The short route through the mud and quicksand that was passing for a building site was covered on foot in my by then lethal work boots which had torn my feet to shreds. I entered the house that was home to the stairwell I was looking for and immediately saw the ladder that we would use to finish our job, back where Glyn was waiting for my return. It didn't quite work that way.

The infamous stairwell was to prove as dangerous as we had all feared, yet it was also to serve me as some kind of bizarre time machine as from then on I can remember nothing.

I had always intended that at some point in my life I would finally achieve my ambitions of making a parachute jump and a bungee jump. At that moment in time, my working tour of Germany came to an abrupt end and both of my ambitions had been achieved at once. However, I had gone one step further down the road of dangerous pastimes by failing to either attach the elastic to my ankles or the parachute to my back. I had chosen instead, albeit unintentionally, to have my fall broken by rock-solid concrete. I do not remember how or why my body began its descent down the stairwell, and it's probably best that I don't. Halfway down, the next floor appeared in the guise of a concrete ledge that was still waiting for the staircase that would join it to the other floors. The advantage of passing that ledge was that it was kind enough to break my fall, the disadvantage being that my head was the only part of my anatomy to crash into that ledge and do all the breaking, in every sense of the word. My then very limp body continued its descent down to the bottom floor where the ground met me.

Meanwhile, back at the wall where Glyn and myself were expected to be working, it wasn't to be too long before Glyn realised that I had been gone too long to be merely skiving and that something may well have been amiss. A search commenced and upon discovering me, he discovered that he was not the first, and promptly joined in with choruses of, 'Get up, you idle bastard!' and other pleasantries.

My failure to take the bait and reply in a similar tone, along with the blood seeping from my ears alerted the gathering above me that the body lying two floors below them was not in fact asleep and that something quite serious had happened. George was next on the scene armed with his mobile phone and by an incredible coincidence, a camera.

'Get an ambulance here and do it fucking now!' was his far from calm request as he thrust his telephone into the hands of a German standing beside him. Curiously, during all the panic, two more Germans had arrived and begun to hastily erect a safety barrier around the offending stairwell. George's camera came in handy and caught their strange behaviour on film for future reference.

In a country world-renowned for its efficiency, it was never going to be a long wait for the ambulance and, sure enough, within minutes, that I am informed felt like hours to all around, one arrived with lights flashing and siren wailing. My then comatose body was gently hoisted out of the well after hasty on the spot treatment by the paramedics and placed into the ambulance which proceeded at speed towards the nearest hospital, my eighth and final set of digs on the Germany '94 tour.

Chapter Six

I Never Liked Christmas Anyway

A state of unconsciousness can sometimes be preferable to being aware of what is going on around you and happening to you. The fact that my head had broken my fall halfway down the well had probably saved my life, yet it had also changed it for ever.

The atmosphere in the Irish Haus that night, or so all of my fellow workers have since told me, was very subdued. I am not entirely sure if this was brought about by worry or by the fact that I had put a dampener on Christmas and in particular the inevitable raucous farewell piss-up we would have enjoyed the night before leaving. I am assured that the latter scenario was not the case and in a strange way, I am almost pleased that it had been me who had quite literally taken the plunge and avoided the feelings that I am told you suffer when you do not have a clue if someone you know is alive or dead. The last that anyone had known was that I was unconscious, bleeding, and being fed into the back of an ambulance at 9 a.m.

Terry had taken the journey to the hospital with me in the back of the ambulance and attempted in vain to glean even the smallest amount of information out of the doctors and nurses who set about treating me at the hospital. The stretcher had been lifted out of the ambulance and whisked away in the maze of corridors within the building. Terry soon realised that he was having the same trouble that had plagued our tour of duty from day one. Even if a doctor could give him an in-depth description of my condition, he would not have understood a word of it and it was hardly the right time or place to try a round of charades, which he was now a master of. Choosing the sensible option, Terry quickly scribbled down his name and the telephone number of the Irish Haus and told the member of staff who had understood his request for the nearest toilet to call him as soon as they had even the tiniest bit of information about the injuries I had suffered.

Terry returned to the digs to inform the rest of the lads that he had found out nothing. At least if a telephone call came the German-speaking owners of the Irish Haus could translate the situation to him. So the wait began, coming to an end early in the afternoon. However, there was no good news about my condition, or for that matter, bad. The fact was there simply wasn't a lot that they could tell Terry or indeed anyone else at that early stage, other than that I had slipped into a coma. Yet another reason for not wanting to be one of the friends involved, was that someone would have to break the news to my family back in England. That unenviable task could still be put off as it would have been wrong to inform everyone that I was in a coma, while not knowing the extent of the injuries that caused me to be in that condition.

When it came to communicating with the Germans, we still hadn't come to terms with saying much beyond 'a beer please' in their own language. It was, however, now clearly necessary to find out as much as possible as quickly as possible. The staff working in the Irish Haus needed to speak good German to survive there. Helen, one of the barmaids employed at the establishment, very kindly volunteered to go to the hospital and find out all she could.

When she returned a couple of hours later, the news she brought back with her to be relayed across the water was not good. The blow to my head had broken my skull, and part of it had forced its way into my brain. Try to imagine pushing your finger through the shell of an egg. Inevitably there will be a small portion of shell that will try to embed itself into the yolk. In the same way, my brain was now attempting to repel a shell-like piece of skull and to a certain extent, failing. The message was this simple. Anyone who cared for me was to get themselves across to the hospital as soon as possible, but even then they may be wasting their time as there was every chance that I may not have been around the following day.

Months later, when I was informed of my family's predicament, I gave a wry smile and went back to what I was thinking about before being rudely interrupted. A year or so later, lying in bed trying to get to sleep, just before reaching that moment when I would drop off, in a moment of total relaxation, complete bliss, and not being aware of anything at all, it dawned on me. In the blink of an eye, a click of the fingers, I was as near to being killed as I cared to think about. The attitude that we all carry with us of, 'it will never happen to me' had proved itself false. It *had* happened, and with a vengeance. I was to have to wait even longer before I could even consider why.

Understandably, Christmas cheer back in England had been replaced by pandemonium. It isn't every day that you are told that your child, brother, sister, lover or friend may well not survive. Outside of my immediate family, Lucy was the first to be informed and she went on to relay the news to all of our friends. My parents and two brothers hastily booked themselves on the next available flight out to Germany and it was agreed that Lucy should be the next to follow – unless the worst happened.

Meanwhile, back on the infamous site, the management were starting to appear concerned but not for my health. It would be far less hassle for them if I were to simply die quickly. The photographs that had been taken by my colleagues did not show the German foreman in a good light. Luckily, they had no idea at all who had taken the shots and there had been plenty of time to whisk away the film before they had even been aware of its existence. None of the lads were questioned about the film's whereabouts. It was better to blame the accident on the cold weather and lay everyone off immediately. 'Go back to England, lads. We will post your wages on.' Surprise, surprise, they never arrived, and nobody expected them to.

Suitcases had been hurriedly packed back home and the atmosphere was very subdued. Nobody had even the slightest idea of what to expect on arrival at the hospital, not even whether I would be alive. Not only were they going to be visiting a loved one who was critically ill, they were going to have to cope with the difficulties of being on foreign soil with nothing pre-arranged and, of course, no one having any knowledge of the area. All of these disturbing thoughts were at the front of everyone's minds by the time the plane touched down at the airport. There was no time to worry and thankfully Terry had decided to postpone his journey home and hang around to meet the sombre-looking group as they made their way into the arrivals lounge. The trip to the hospital was to be an easy one, with a fellow Brit in tow, who knew the area and could act as their guide.

Leipzig is a beautiful old city and a drive through it for a first-time visitor is an enjoyable one. Not on that occasion. The fifteen-minute journey passed by with everyone totally oblivious to their surroundings. The first time that any of the group except Terry became aware of where they were was when the hospital appeared ahead. Standing in front of

Terry and my family only minutes after walking out of Leipzig airport and climbing into a taxi was an old building of some size which appeared to be the product of an argument between two architects. One had wanted the building to resemble a town hall and the other had been convinced that he was designing a home for very old and possibly disturbed patients.

Now that everyone had digested the 'splendour' of the building it was time to take a deep breath and hope that they would find me looking better than had been described over the telephone. First impressions of my general state were not good. The blow to my head had blackened both my eyes and the rest of my body was cut, grazed and not wholly healthy, not to mention a very nasty swelling at the side of my head. Not to be outdone by her son, my mother promptly hit the floor quicker than I had thirty-six hours previously!

There is not a lot anyone can do when the patient who they are visiting isn't even aware of their presence. All you can do is sit and stare, slowly becoming more depressed and upset. Eventually, after a few hours a nurse appeared bringing along with her an adequate knowledge of the English language and tried her very best to explain everything to my visitors. Brain damage is an injury, the effects of which are difficult, almost impossible to predict. Being comatose only adds to the confusion. I had struck the right-hand side of my head and as explained previously a piece of skull was lodged precariously on my brain. There was a fifty-fifty chance that the rogue piece of bone would work its way back into its rightful position without any intervention. If this did not happen the only other option was to open up my head and take matters in hand.

I am actually delighted to have been in the coma at that time. On hearing of the possibility of having my head opened up like a box, I would surely have sped up the whole process no end by simply dying there and then of the medical cowardice that runs in torrents through my veins. In a case involving injuries such as my own, you can forgot all of the fancy terminology that nobody outside of the medical profession understands. Just one single word is all that's needed – time. Nothing more. Would my skull see fit to right itself without the need for surgery? Time. Would I wake up and look around once more? Time. Would I ever be aware of who the people around me were? Time. At that point in the proceedings it was all very easy for me, not so for the concerned onlookers. I may as well have been on another planet as everyone worried about whether I would ever awaken and what to expect if I did. Unfortunately, there was still a lot more to contemplate before any of the thoughts revolved around my awakening.

Soon after my family's arrival, permission was sought by the doctors to perform a tracheotomy to do my breathing for me whilst I was attached to the life-support machine. My father did not have to think long and hard about the decision. If you are asked to let someone make it easy for your son to breathe, you are highly unlikely to say no. Within an hour a hole had been made in my throat and the tube inserted into one of those wounds that look so painful when you see somebody else lying in a hospital bed in a similar situation. Thank God for comas! It never looked painful to me, as I never saw it. After having the air pipe attached to the motor, next came the fuel pipe to keep it running smoothly. Yet another tube entered my body and only the means of escape for the used fuel remained. Two smaller pipes appeared in uncomfortable parts of my anatomy and all of a sudden the visiting experience became a more traumatic time for everyone. Not many people have any desire to visit a friend who spends his entire day in the lavatory or even worse, choosing to use a plastic bag situated next to their bed in full view of all and sundry.

A very tiresome day for the family eventually came to an end and they faced the daunting prospect of having no bed for the night. For obvious reasons my sleeping quarters back at the Irish Haus had been vacated and so with the promise of a second bed my two brothers found their accommodation without even having to look. The boisterous building site mentality of the place ruled my parents out of that particular solution but soon another opportunity presented itself.

The hospital had seen the likes of English builders before but rarely one who had required treatment more serious than an X-ray and a plaster cast. The staff had found themselves in new territory, caring for an Englander in their intensive care unit. They had found that within two days of my arrival they had been surrounded by English visitors. The whole experience was a novelty for the former East Germans and they seemed to enjoy the attention. For that reason I soon had celebrity status in the hospital. The nurse who had earlier greeted my family, using as much of the English language as she knew, returned to check on the star of the show. Learning of the bedless predicament that my parents found themselves in, within a minute she decided that they would stay with her for the duration of their stay. Even if the answer had been no to her kind offer, it would not have been accepted. She was adamant that not a single coin would be leaving their pockets throughout their time in Leipzig. She would do absolutely everything that it was humanly possible to do to make their visit as easy and painless as it could be.

Along with her kindness, her knowledge of events at the hospital made her a very useful acquaintance to have. It wasn't to be too long before the word 'acquaintance' was not a true reflection on the woman and was quickly replaced by 'friend'. Claudia, as she introduced herself, led the two strangers back to her abode and introduced them to the rest of her family who, like Claudia, did all they could to make them feel welcome – a gesture of unbelievable kindness that would never be forgotten and gave them comfort and escape from the trauma for a brief moment or two. After all, they could have been unlucky and been forced to sleep at the train station, thereby joining an exclusive club already boasting their son as a member!

Two days of contrast between upsetting periods of worry and stunning German hospitality dragged on towards their inevitable conclusion, finally ending with many tears, hugs and kisses at Claudia's home. A final beer at the Irish Haus and one final visit to my now familiar bedside loomed for my two brothers before climbing into the taxi to Leipzig airport with my parents. Being in a coma and therefore totally oblivious to all that is happening around you has two distinct advantages. The first is that goodbyes aren't nearly so tearful. The second, and most important, is that I was never aware that I was to be left totally alone apart from the nurses who couldn't even speak to me in my own language. It was financially impossible for any member of my family to stay with me indefinitely. After all, nobody knew how long I would be there.

Despite the fact that I was in a period of unintentional rest with no awareness at all of the events happening around me, friends were being made for life. News of my accident had travelled at a frightening pace through both Terry and George and my only visitors for the next few days were to be Christian, Basti and Romy, three foreigners who only two months previously had been total strangers. This fact did not seem to bother them at all as they soon organised a system in which they all took turns to sit for hours next to my bed, hold my hand, and talk any old rubbish that came to their minds in an attempt to get a response from my apparently lifeless body.

One of my intentions now to bring a smile to the face of anyone unfortunate enough to have been in a coma is to invent a recording device which will save for posterity every word uttered by the people at their bedsides. I am sure that some of the recording would be sad and tearful, but there would be an awful lot to laugh at too. One of these recordings would have given me a great deal of pleasure in the days that would follow my eventual return. Included would have been every word of half-German, half-English spoken by my German friends, along with the attempts of my two brothers to stir me by recreating my liking of the music of Queen and delivering to me and anyone else within earshot a woefully out-of-tune version of 'Bohemian Rhapsody'.

Meanwhile, back in the real world, Lucy was still incredibly worried and the news being relayed to her was not very reassuring. Stories of a black and blue body, feeding tubes, catheters and tracheotomies rarely conjure up an image of your loved one that you wish to see. She decided that it would be best for her to get on a plane and go and see me for herself. Not wishing to make the upsetting trip alone, her sister agreed to tag along with her. Claudia, on hearing of their impending arrival, immediately stopped any worries they may have had about the cost of staying in a hotel, and offered the comforts of her own home for as long as they were to stay – yet another show of incredible kindness from one of our new-found friends and the sort of treatment that had long since ceased to amaze anyone. There was never any doubt that the German hand of friendship would be waiting for whoever decided to make the trip.

Had the accident occurred back in my own country, it seems an inappropriate word to use but the whole saga would have been much 'easier' not only for me but also for the rest of my family. An ambulance would have arrived within minutes and whisked me off to the nearest hospital.

My treatment would have started immediately and continued until all the medics around saw fit to send me home. The doctors and nurses would have been able to understand everything that I said to them and, more importantly, I would have understood them. Similarly, all my friends and family would have been immediately aware of what had happened and the injuries that I had suffered. Then they could all jump into a car and visit me as soon as they could, and as often as they could thereafter. When I returned to consciousness, I would have known that at least one person that I knew well could visit me every day of my stay. Finally, on my eventual discharge I would have been home in twenty uneventful minutes. However, to complicate matters even more, with any form of head injury flying is a problem – yet another problem for the doctors and my family to consider.

Lucy finally arrived at the hospital, unsure of what to expect. I was still deep in a coma but, thankfully, some good news did await. The piece of skull that had lodged itself on my brain had reset itself without the need for a chisel, scalpel and copious amounts of anaesthetic. For obvious reasons, this was not exactly staggering news for me at the time yet it was news that would eventually aid my recovery. I am sure that the emotional scars would have taken a lot longer to heal had I been reminded of them every time I was to stare into a mirror and witness the evidence.

This piece of news was a pleasant greeting for Lucy, yet there was still precious little that anybody could tell her regarding what to expect if and when I was to open my eyes. It is virtually impossible to predict the consequences of a brain injury while the patient is still unconscious. Only when they are able to move and communicate can the full extent of the damage be assessed. There are so many different factors to take into account, starting with how many millions of vital parts of the brain had been affected.

Most of us who have never undergone any form of medical treatment or paid any attention to the plague of hospital dramas on TV are ignorant of the effects of a serious head injury. The reality is that the injured person is walking down a frightening corridor that only has three doors to escape through. All three doors have a clearly marked sign. The first door says in bright letters 'seriously disabled'. Further down the corridor, the second reads 'long, slow haul' and finally there is the third option, the most sought after, 'lucky bastard'. Unfortunately, you are unable to choose for yourself and it is simply a matter of waiting to see through which exit you emerge.

The only hint of what I had to expect was that the right-hand side of my brain had taken the full force of the impact. This meant that it was to be the left side of my body which would suffer if I was to awaken, due to the curious way in which the brain works, similar to a photo-graphic negative. I would not of course have any serious problems should I be fortunate enough to exit through that door marked 'lucky bastard'. If you are fortunate enough to find that exit you hurry through at such speed that you fail to take any note of the ominous-looking asterisk next to the name on the sign. A look at the small print below will show that one in every twenty people who suffer any form of head injury may eventually develop epilepsy. One in twenty is a small enough percentage for me personally not to have worried about it anyway, because – 'it'll never happen to me. Ha!'

The thousands of possible outcomes were not even en-tering Lucy's head as she sat with her sister, desperately trying to think of something to say to my still comatose body. It was their turn to just sit and watch, and sit and watch, etc. The only event to break up the day was observing how many times I was to visit the lavatory in a prone position – not really anyone's idea of a fun day out. Lucy was quite obviously not enjoying the experience, but her hurt had been softened by my ability to clear all of my debts only days before the plunge. All of her money was back in its purse and I had, in effect, become loveable again at just the right time. It was perhaps not the best reason to be visiting but I am sure I appreciated it and the desire to live and the jubilation at escaping my close call would blind me to reality in the days, weeks and months following my return, clouding my judgement.

It is impossible to observe what the people around you are doing, either good or bad when comatose. When your eyes finally open and everything once again is visible to you, nothing makes any sense. You have no recollection of events and even the darker aspects of people's behaviour around you fail to register as your brain struggles to cope with the massive influx of information in a short space of time. In effect, you are just as blind as you were when blissfully unaware of your surroundings before. Once again, the word 'time' is important. As I remained ignorant to all around me, the minutes turned to hours and the hours eventually turned into the two days that Lucy had planned to stay, an uneventful two days with no noticeable change

in my condition. On the morning of the second day Claudia had been thanked for her kindness and the final visit to my bedside climaxed in a tearful farewell.

By that time Christmas was only three days away and the prospects of me doing any celebrating were decidedly remote. However, my celebrity status had not been reserved for just the hospital staff. Some of them had obviously told their families about the Englander whose trip to Germany had gone badly wrong. The daughter of a nurse caring for me had brought along a Christmas decoration that she made at school and hung it upon the drip feed as her way of wishing me a Happy Christmas and Good Health! I am positive that had the accident happened in any other area of the world other than East Germany I would not have received half the attention that the people gave me in that hospital in Leipzig. My fall had occurred at exactly the right time as everybody in the city was trying their very best to westernise themselves as quickly as they possibly could. Having one small group of English people who had known no other way since birth visiting the hospital to see me was a novelty and one that I am sure they enjoyed. The chance to spend time with people who were bored with everything that they were only beginning to see was too good to miss.

Christmas Day arrived. If somebody had looked in a crystal ball five years previously and foreseen that I would be oblivious to the whole of the festive season in '94, I would have assumed that it could only be due to over-indulgence in alcohol. Surely nothing else would make me quite so unwilling to participate in any form of celebration? I would have been wrong, very wrong – in fact an awfully long way wide of the mark. Christmas is traditionally the time of year that you spend socialising with your family, but that year was to be different. The rest of the family had to return home and I was on my own. All that my family and friends could do was to raise a glass to me and pray for my recovery. Any smiles were difficult to find as everyone sat and waited for even the tiniest ray of hope; a single eye flickering would have been enough.

On the morning of Christmas Day Christian made one of his regular visits to see me in an attempt to gain a response from me and also to make sure that I did receive at least one visitor at Yuletide, something that was not to be appreciated by me until the following Christmas – only then did it sink in how much I appreciated his selfless act.

Needless to say, despite all of his efforts to communicate with me, I remained unconscious and unresponsive. If I had failed to show any awareness of Romy's presence days beforehand, then the chances of Christian getting a response hovered precariously between slim and none at all. After three hours of trying, the latter proved to be true and Christian departed to spend the rest of the day with his family.

Maybe Boxing Day would be the one that saw me return to consciousness. Maybe the memory of having a damn good time back at home would spark a flicker of emotion in my mind, see me awaken and strive to recover. After all, there are not many days in the year when you are almost guaranteed not to have to work and enjoy the day instead. Boxing Day is one of the few. Had my awareness of time disappeared completely, or despite being comatose was my body clock still ticking? If my batteries were low, then they would either run out completely or simply need recharging. If they were to run out then it would eventually be a silent goodbye. If they only needed recharging I would eventually awake and spend time recovering. It could take days, weeks or even years.

Unfortunately, as with fixing anything that has broken, it is unlikely that it will ever work as well as it had when it was new. The question was, if I awoke how close to the original would I be? I was still alive, but what were the extent of my injuries? What adjustments would I have to make, if any? There was every chance that I could go through the rest of my life functioning perfectly or, like driving a car, I may experience one or two of those annoying rattles, the source of which, you can never quite pinpoint.

Boxing Day '94 started with very much the same routine as the day before. Christian entered the hospital and headed for the ward in search of his friend who had been lying motionless in bed for three weeks. He sat down and prepared himself for another frustrating hour or so. Again he received no response on greeting me and began to relay to me what had happened in his life in the hours since his last visit.

Then – *shock*! Midway through one of Christian's tales of Christmas drunkenness, two eyes slowly opened and he almost fell off his chair. I may as well have been still comatose as I had no idea of who or what was sat next to me and simply stared blankly at whatever it was. My batteries *had* needed recharging and my body clock had begun to tick again. A wake-up alarm had sounded in my mind, my eyes had opened and a loud 'Whoop!' rang around the ward.

Christian immediately rushed off to find a telephone and relay the good news back to England. The long-awaited call was taken and a loud 'Whoop!' rang around my home too. Various calls were made to inform everyone of the news and several loud 'Whoops!' rang around the homes of Lucy and the rest of my friends. Celebratory drinks were most definitely called for and the till in my local watering hole loudly 'Whooped!' as the money flowed through it at a quite startling rate.

Christian returned to my bedside with a smile on his face and sat himself down to await the next development. Although the fact that I had opened my eyes was not in itself very spectacular, to all concerned it was a major milestone and the next wasn't long in coming. Christian grasped my hand and proceeded to ask me if I knew who he was. I had no idea. He could have been from Jupiter for all I knew, but I apparently squeezed his hand. This was proof to all concerned that I at least had some awareness of my surroundings, a huge step but one that didn't seem of great value to me at the time.

To everybody who had been worried since that day on the site it must have felt like the end of a long road. As I was soon to learn, these first signs were just the beginning for me of a long and arduous journey. It was as if I was in a car, driving aimlessly, with no knowledge of where I was heading or what I would do when I got there. At that precise moment in time, I was simply lost. I had successfully avoided the road heading down and was trying to find the exit that led to the comfort of my own home. It was a complicated road with various exits and how I stayed on it was up to me alone. There was far too much to consider before the going would become any easier. I could easily just be driving to the shops for a packet of cigarettes, but the law of averages meant that there was just as much chance of me going on one long tour of the motorways, a very long and arduous journey that would eventually take the word 'tedium' to unexplored heights. If only tedium had been my only concern! But for now it was to be a long time before I would be fully conscious and aware of any of the delights that the German specialists had in store for me.

The six weeks following my awakening are still a blur when only the painful highlights stand out clearly in my mind. Life was simply total and utter confusion. Before any memories I can recall clearly, I must have had no idea who I was, why I was in the strange, sterile-smelling building and trying desperately to work out who the faces staring at me belonged to. All of this was explained to me numerous times by doctors and visitors to my bedside, but unfortunately my brain could not store the information for any length of time. I could not make any sense of my circumstances and the arrival of friends and family who had flown over just to visit me in my hour of need failed to register at all. My parents were the first to hotfoot it over the water again to be at my bedside and arrived to a similar greeting to the one that they had when I was comatose – a blank expression and staring eyes that did not give the impression that I was happy to see them. I wasn't. I couldn't see them in my head although my eyes were functioning normally.

On that visit it was the turn of Christian to offer hospitality, giving the full use of his flat, a short tram ride from the hospital. Romy met my parents at the airport and escorted them to hospital, neither of them being aware that they were sitting opposite the woman of my dreams. My father later told me that although he was a sprightly sixty-year-old, I would have had to fight him to the death for the gorgeous one's affections. I was confident that a forty-year-older version of myself would not hold quite the same attraction for her as I did, should she ever be foolish enough to want to find out. Unfortunately for both of us, she never did, but I'll die waiting anyway! At that particular moment in time my father was certainly holding the upper hand as the choice was between one mature, financially comfortable male and a bedridden adult with no recollection of the people around him and a tendency, I'm told, to turn very nasty very quickly.

It is also tremendously difficult to look attractive when you are lying on a bed with only your vital parts covered, staring into space, with various tubes protruding from man-made orifices about your person, some of which were draining your bodily fluids. Add to this the fact that I wasn't exactly up to intelligent conversation and you were left with somebody who was hardly desirable to the opposite sex!

I am sure that this was something that Lucy was trying to cope with on her visits, although she did seem to be handling all the stress well. It was, however, very early days. All of your stress vanishes pretty quickly when someone you are close to has survived a close call, awoken from a coma and looks as if they will make some sort of recovery. It is then down to the individual as to how he or she will handle the long recovery period of the patient, when he must come to terms with his injuries, while trying to make sense of how he got into the situation initially.

Everybody handles this period of recovery differently, as do the people around them. It may soon become much more difficult than anticipated as it becomes clear that the injured person may not be making the recovery that everyone expected within weeks of being discharged. The process can creep well past weeks into months and years. Some of your loved ones may well be with you every step of the way, although after the initial honeymoon period when everyone is delighted that you have survived, the period of rehabilitation is a different matter. They are no longer dealing with the same person, either mentally or physically, as the one who had the accident weeks before. This fact on its own is difficult to accept. Add to it the twenty-four hour a day lethargy and the problems that can go along with any form of damage to the brain and slowly the euphoria dies, to be replaced by the knowledge that the coming months are going to be anything but easy.

You can be very fortunate and have everyone close to you wanting to help and be around to give their support, or they can just drift away, unable to come to terms with the situation. I was foolish enough to automatically assume that everyone I knew would fall into the helpful category, but there is always that tiny minority and they would eventually surface in the near future. I would have happily wagered huge sums of money on some people's constant support remaining with me for years, but I had still not quite learnt to see those slaps in the face coming!

Chapter Seven

Friends for Life

My parents were understandably oblivious to anything other than my immediate well-being as they continued to sit at my bedside and wait for the smallest indication I was aware of who they were. It must have been a difficult and traumatic time when the lad they had carefully brought up failed to recognise them and stared through them in an almost frightening manner. I will probably never have any recollection of those early post-comatose days, which is probably for the best to save me any embarrassment. As I slowly became aware of my surroundings and who was visiting me, I still failed to remember how to behave in the company of my parents. Respect was not a word in my vocabulary. The odd threat coupled with a smattering of language fresh from the building site and a tendency towards violence were all part of my less than engaging personality as I made my way from that corridor, trying to establish which of those three doors I had exited by. I had strolled past the 'seriously disabled' door and smashed my way out somewhere between 'long slow haul' and 'lucky bastard' and the ultimate direction was still far from clear.

The next six weeks of my stay at 'Hotel Krankenhaus' are nothing but a total blur in my mind. My parents visited twice, as did Lucy; my elder brother once, as he had family commitments, the other three; Romy three times; and Christian was present at least every other day and I remember a grand total of approximately five minutes of his company throughout the ordeal.

My brother's third visit was to be the eventual end of that desolate area of my memory. I had slowly become more and more aware of his presence through the duration of his visit. Eventually the few words that I was uttering began to form sentences and further still into slow, deliberate but comprehensible conversations. Most of my conversations though were very repetitive as I had this obsession that a taxi could be called and I would simply walk away – understandable, but nonsensical!

The morning before my brother's departure arrived and he paid his usual visit to see me, but this time he was not alone. Closely behind, brandishing a hot cheeseburger from the local takeaway and grinning his usual ten-mile-wide smile was George, extremely nervous and unsure of what to expect. When all you know is that your friend has suffered brain damage, I assume every possibility must go through your mind, both good and bad. It's always the worst case scenarios that take hold of your thoughts. 'He will be paralysed' or 'severely injured' and a picture of my limp body sat in a wheelchair were just some of the pleasant things that the people who knew me but had not seen me since the accident had been imagining and George was no different.

Since those never to be forgotten words, 'I'll go and fetch a ladder, Glyn', I had spent three weeks comatose coupled with a further three spent in an empty void. George and my brother's entry into that void with the soon devoured cheeseburger is my first clear memory. I had reached the summit of my climb, but then plummeted down the hill into that void of memory, continually. I would remember the occasional five-minute period and then nothing, again and again. It was total confusion for myself and everyone concerned. The euphoria of your friend or relative's survival soon fades away when the panic subsides and then you realise that they are not going to be back to their best for some time, if ever.

It is an easy trap to fall into. After all of the waiting and worrying, suddenly your loved one is back, back for good and obviously fully recovered. He is still alive so he must be. Unfortunately, that only happens rarely and it is only a matter of time before reality hits home and the longer everybody fails to realise, the more painful the blow is. The friend or member of the family concerned appears to be the same person on the outside, yet no matter how subtle the changes are, there may still be changes. Those surrounding the patient will never understand and come to terms with the changes until the injured person has seen them and they could be in for a long wait.

'What changes?'

'No, I am not.'

'No, I was not.'

'What are you talking about?'

'It is not me who has changed!'

They are still fresh in my mind.

During George's visit, I would be awake and alert briefly and then fail to know who he or anyone else around me actually were. More than one person has since commented on my ability at that time to sit perfectly still and stare into space or right through my visitor in an unnerving manner.

George was the first to struggle with this situation. Just six weeks earlier we had successfully negotiated all of the aforementioned struggles that inevitably occur when working in another country. At the time they had seemed hard going but now they were just a part of the smallest drop in the ocean. We had settled into life in Germany and made some great friends on the sites and at Christian's club. Even the longest working days had begun to be less of a struggle. All of the lads got on well together and our days were never short of a few laughs. Unfortunately, all of the pluses had turned into one huge minus on that cold morning and now George was talking to his friend who only barely recognised him – difficult and upsetting. I hope I never have to find out for myself how much. What I do know is that the victim of a serious head injury has a far easier ride in the early stages following the accident than his friends and relatives. From day one I had only one choice, to sit back and enjoy the ride while desperately trying to learn from each twist and turn that my injuries put me through. It was the people around me who suffered as they witnessed my struggles.

Meanwhile, back at my bedside, reality was beginning to dawn on George who was attempting to jog my memory by telling me of tales from the site whilst all the time goading me with an unopened packet of cigarettes. I didn't take the bait, as I couldn't care less about smoking. Being hospitalised for six weeks does that to you, although I wouldn't recommend it as the easiest method of quitting! The lack of any response shocked George who before the accident had become used to us having a laugh at each other's expense, the cigarettes being a cruel extension that I would have undoubtedly used had the shoe been on the other foot.

The visit seemed to be more upsetting for George than for any members of my family or circle of friends. Most of my family and friends had had the time to try and accept what they found in the hospital. However, George was a newcomer and the experience was not proving easy for him. My brother had, after all, spent most of his time since my return to the land of the living sitting next to me experiencing the frustrations that come from trying to communicate with someone who only occasionally understands what you are saying and even then, speaks nothing but complete rubbish. Throughout this, the patient he had been visiting had appeared to be exactly the same person that he had grown up with, apart from a drastic weight loss. All of that, coupled with his intense dislike of needles which he shared with my father and other brother, not to mention myself, and indeed dislike of hospitals in general had made his visits tremendously arduous.

I was now conscious, but my awareness was far from one hundred per cent. Much like life in general, I would only now and again understand what was happening to me and realise that something sterile and razor sharp was about to enter my body.

During these brief moments my brother was in effect my crutch, but there was always going to come a time when no matter how much he wanted to leave the hospital with me, his wife and work commitments would make it impossible for him to stay any longer and that time had now come. It would prove to be far harder for him to leave than it was for me to witness his departure. After all, he knew what was happening. He did have one more day to spend with me and his departure would be made that little bit easier by the arrival of George, who had turned up unannounced and informed my brother that after his impending trip to see Christian at the club he would return to ensure that I wasn't alone. Half of the worry for everybody involved was that I would be lying for days on end surrounded by nothing familiar or understandable to me while undergoing continued treatment. George's stay would allay those fears in the short term. Being confined to a hospital bed is stressful to all concerned but when yourself and all of your loved ones are absolutely positive that you are not even going to be able to have a conversation with the nurses tending to your needs, as none of them understand a word you are saying, then that's yet another worry. That part of my hospital stay is one that I remember clearly and will never forget. It is impossible to describe accurately the feelings of frustration that I encountered every morning as I awoke to find myself still in a ward with only faces. My frustration would turn into desperation by afternoon every single day. Every so often the faces would speak to break the monotony, but only one word in every hundred was understandable to me. Each day was identical to the previous one: awake, food, wash, injection, sleep, toilet, wash, food, injection, tablet, sleep, sleep and more sleep! My desperation soon escalated into sheer hatred for the faces that were planning my exciting daily routine. The mornings were always the most uplifting part of the day as for just a few seconds after I awoke I would fail to realise just exactly where I was. As reality dawned it became clear that yet another day had been successfully negotiated and I was one nearer to returning home. If I never saw that damned bed again it would be too soon, I would think and then wait for the next day.

I was still unsure of the seriousness of my condition which had forced me to call a sterile mattress 'home' for such an uncomfortable amount of time. My yearning for home was now virtually uncontrollable. Friends, family, my own bed, edible food and just the good old English language were playing very strongly in my mind. All of those thoughts were not making me much fun to be around. I *had* to get home and was positive that I would eventually persuade someone to throw me out if that was what it would take to escape!

On the final day of my brother's visit, after an hour of failing to get anything other than talk of home delivered in an inane babble he eventually gave in and made his way out of the ward on one of his 'tea breaks'. That particular one seemed to last for an age. It transpired that his break had consisted of him finding the nearest payphone and pleading with my parents to 'get him out of there'. Unfortunately, it wasn't that easy. Numerous pleas to the local MP, European MP, and finally cutting out the middleman and writing directly to the House of Commons had resulted in nothing. I hadn't merely broken a limb, I had done the job properly by breaking my skull, thereby making flying something of a problem. With a serious head injury any pressure placed on the skull is potentially very dangerous and so stepping on to an aeroplane in my condition was not a good idea without any medical help nearby. Therefore the only means of getting me home would have been by chartering an air ambulance with medics on board. That option was checked out immediately and found to cost somewhere in the region of a small Third-World country's debt, a little on the expensive side for an average working family who, after numerous pleas for some financial help, had got precisely nowhere and so all of my brother's pleas were in vain. The only option remaining was to lie and wait until the doctors decided that it was safe for me to travel and wave me off for good. Yet again, time was the keyword. It could take days or it could take weeks.

My brother arrived that night for what was to be his final visit with George following close behind. His flight was scheduled for the early hours of the following morning. I know that should I be faced with the same predicament again I would feel very nervous and tremendously upset at the thought of being left alone for an unknown amount of time, in a strange land with little understanding of my plight. Luckily, it didn't seem quite so bad at the time. My lack of understanding was the reason. Every day that went by involved me being positive that the next would be the one that I had been waiting for and I never thought that I would be alone for too long. That state of minor euphoria wouldn't last all day though, and as the minutes ticked by, the boredom would slowly kick in. By that time, the reality was starting to stick in my mind. Everything that had occurred forty-eight hour earlier would be buried in the void that was passing itself off as my memory. The extent of my injuries was, however, starting to imbed itself in my mind. I still was not quite able to work out how I had come to be saddled with the injuries in the first place. Had something struck my head, was my predicament self-inflicted, had I been on the receiving end of some German aggression or had I simply enjoyed myself too much one night?

The hours leading up to my brother's departure passed by quickly. My own lack of emotion at his impending disappearance was not shared as he became noticeably more and more agitated as the afternoon merged into one with every other afternoon spent in the hospital. Everybody was still in the dark when it came to the question of my transfer to a rehabilitation unit in England. Leipzig hospital would still be my official residence for some time to come.

Was this visit to be his last in Germany? It certainly was for some time as finances were running low. Needless to say, I was oblivious to the amount of visits that had been made by my parents, my brothers, my friends and Lucy – if she had ever been I had no idea at all. I could remember five minutes previously. Five days? Not a chance. She had, in fact, been twice I was to learn later, much to my surprise.

The time for tearful farewells arrived. My last contact with home left, only to return briefly in order for two grown men to hug each other and then he was gone. Only George remained, but I was destined never to see him in Germany again, despite the fact that he had promised my family that he would be ever-present at my bedside for at least a week after his arrival. His promise was never to be fulfilled. He had visited expecting to find the same cheerful builder who had been working with him before the accident. He would walk in, sit down, share some jokes and soon forget just how ill I was. That was his problem – he had failed to realise that I had anything other than a nasty bout of flu and the reality hit him hard. Hard enough for him to walk away and not return. Everybody reacts to situations in a different way and he simply could not handle what he saw; it frightened him. Immediately my family jumped on the 'How could he!' band wagon, and I thought the same as I waited and waited. But we could not see the situation through his eyes and begin to understand his emotions. We were in no position to start wagging fingers, although we would all like everyone to think and behave exactly as we would ourselves.

Unfortunately, it never quite works like that and you have to try and understand how other people are feeling. What one person finds easy to cope with, another can find exactly the opposite and that is what had happened. He simply could not come to terms with what everyone who had visited before had actually managed to deal with. It seemed callous to all concerned, yet the only option for George was to turn and walk away. Sometimes, no matter what is said to some people, it is easier for them to block it all out and continue to concern themselves with their own problems, no matter how small.

After the unexpected walk-out, what everyone had been dreading was then upon me. George's promises had come to nothing and I was facing an unknown period of time in the hospital with no familiar visitors who could break up the monotony of trying my hardest to learn German from what fellow patients and staff were saying to me, and quickly giving up. An hour later, I would try again with the same outcome, etc. The only visitor I was to receive in those next few days was Christian who would always visit during his stays in Leipzig. Those visits would be infrequent, but appreciated as much as any visit during the whole stay.

Afterwards Christian would report back to England if he felt my condition had improved noticeably and eventually I reached a level where I was able to receive and fully appreciate telephone calls from home. They were calls of no great length, as I tired very easily and it was difficult to find a suitable topic of conversation. I had no idea of what was going on in the world outside and cared even less.

One particular day stands out clearly in my mind. It was a day that started out as routinely as ever – awake, food, wash, sleep, awake and spend ten minutes trying to work out where the hell I was again. Occasionally, throughout the day one of the many nurses would amble into the ward clutching a telephone as a patient had received a call. On that particular day, a nurse bearing an uncanny resemblance to an Olympic shot-putter marched in and the call was for me. I reached across and grabbed the telephone, yanking it from her vicelike grip with a strong sense of urgency. Awaiting me on the other end of the line was Lucy. My subdued 'Hello' made its way down the line to England to be answered with an extremely cheerful greeting from the other end. Although Lucy had visited me twice in hospital, the telephone call was the first time that I had spoken to her that I could remember since the call on my birthday, five days before the accident. To anyone who knew me back then I must have sounded slightly ignorant as I had very little interest in anything at all that my friends and relatives had to say. I just wanted to be left alone. On his many visits, Christian would arrive and by the time the greetings were over and done with, I had had enough and was ready for him to leave. It was exactly the same with many of the telephone calls that started to come in; I couldn't think of anything to say. It was pointless telling everyone that I was all right, because I clearly wasn't. The conversation with Lucy followed the same path as many of the calls I received, barely a minute long containing nothing worthwhile being said by either of us. After a very brief conversation we exchanged 'I love you's and the call came to an end with me momentarily forgetting it had ever happened.

Ten minutes after Lucy's attempted conversation, the shot-putter returned clutching the telephone and yet again heading in my direction. The phone was placed next to my ear and a quiet voice said, 'Hi, Andy, it's Romy.' All of a sudden I was wide awake and alert. That was to be the first in a long line of calls, almost one daily, made by a concerned friend who could speak the same language and knew that it would be sweet music to my ears at that time. It certainly was and her kindness shown to a foreigner who she had known for only a few weeks was very much appreciated. It was also to continue for many weeks following my eventual discharge.

Those calls along with the visits of Christian undoubtedly went a long way towards speeding up my recovery. It would have been very easy to see me awake and think that their work was done. Those visits and calls from my German friends seemed to mean more to me at the time than those from England. It was as if I expected the attention from England and anything else was a bonus. Expected? That was to be my downfall in the months to come.

A coma is simply being oblivious to everything. When the eyes open, the shock of what you wake up to is frightening. Total separation from what you know isn't wise, especially when you awake and discover that a lot of what you know has altered drastically. The brain is a complex organ at the best of times and cannot be expected to take in such a large amount of information and make sense of it in just a few minutes. It was going to take possibly years, depending on my injuries, to make any sort of recovery. The immediate problem however was simple. I had to spend the days concentrating and trying to return my mind to the state that it had been in prior to the accident – perhaps not the best mind in the world, but my own nevertheless.

The keyword here as it is with recovery from any kind of accident, be it serious or merely a cut finger, is wait. It was impossible with the kind of injuries that I had sustained to try and remember. You cannot sit alone and attempt to force yourself into having memories. All that happened in your life will eventually force its way back into your mind if you are lucky. This period of time is made a whole lot easier by simply talking to the people you know. Just one sentence can be enough to nudge one memory out of its hiding place. For that reason alone, any contact with my German friends was a massive help in the times when no members of my family or my circle of friends could be with me. The more conversation you have, the more familiar you become with what has happened and what is happening.

Two, three, maybe even four days passed by. I neither knew nor cared. Every day was the same as the next and only the odd phone call would punctuate the routine. Lucy had now started to sound upset during our brief telephone calls, distraught to the point of tears on one occasion – that I remember clearly. My lack of consciousness on her first visit and lack of sanity on the second meant that I had not one single recollection of her visits. That alone must be upsetting enough for the visitor without having to confront the various problems that their loved one may have. The more I spoke to Lucy and heard her concern, the more I yearned almost painfully for what to me felt like escape. Two conversations ended with me in tears. I needed to get home, desperately. I was craving for that almost as much as I was for the cigarettes which I was not able to have.

Barely a minute after one particularly upsetting conversation with a clearly distraught Lucy, an unknown doctor appeared at my bedside sporting one of those cheesy 'I'm going to hurt you' smiles that medics always adopt in an attempt to disguise what's coming next. They never quite succeed. He proceeded to pull the sheets on my bed down to my waist and began to view the tube which at that time had been protruding from my stomach for eight weeks. He placed what appeared to be cream on to the wound and started to mumble incoherently to me in German. That was something that I had become very used to over my stay, but that time I couldn't even begin to understand some of the words being used. I had no idea at all what the man was saying or doing. For all I knew, he could have been a man off the street, wearing a white coat and having a cruel joke at my expense. I had struggled to understand what had been said to me by the other doctors who I saw every day. A doctor who was a stranger to me was wasting his time though if he thought that I had even the tiniest clue what he was talking about. That was just one of the problems that was making the entire hospital experience a complete nightmare. Being in hospital for a long time is difficult enough at the best of times, but when your only option is to try and guess what everyone around you dressed in white is warning you about, you tend to become even more nervous as all sorts of horrors swirl around in your head, most of them a hell of a lot worse than what is actually coming. I remember thinking on more than one occasion that I was definitely going to die in Germany.

The anonymous doctor seemed to be aware of the language barrier and the problems it was causing. He decided to try and slip in a word of English here and there to enable me to have a better idea of what to look forward to. A long monologue had been delivered by the time the word 'endoscope' was slipped into a sentence. The doctor grinned proudly as he was now certain that at long last someone had been able to communicate with me. Unfortunately, he hadn't taken into account that I had previously struggled desperately to recall who the strangers at my bedside were and if I failed to recognise my family and friends, then it was certain I was always going to have difficulty with phrases of a medical nature, as I probably hadn't even known them in the first place. I slipped back down into my usual prone position and proceeded to worry about the vasectomy that I might be having that day. It wasn't long before that particular fear was blown away.

The pining for home once again hit me and I had long since stopped trying to work out what was in store for me when four nurses arrived, gave me a quick wash down, took their positions at each corner of the bed, and at pace began to wheel my bed out of the ward and into the maze of corridors winding through the hospital. Throughout my whole sightseeing trip around the hospital, I was unaware of the whole point of the journey and the destination that I was heading for. For reasons known only to the specialists treating me they had chosen to keep me in the dark about what they were going to do. However, I was not worrying as we finally came to a halt after a five-minute journey. Although I was still hospitalised, the change of scenery was very uplifting. The familiar four walls that had surrounded me for weeks had been briefly replaced by a fresh set of walls. I had never known how much personal pleasure could be gained by simply staring at a wall. I had memorised every nook and cranny of the four walls back in the ward – apart from meals and telephone calls there was little else to do. The new set of bricks and mortar that had me consumed with interest were conveniently blotting out my concern for what was happening. I still had no knowledge of what the doctor had meant by the word 'endoscope' when he had spoken to me earlier and I was still half expecting him to perform the vasectomy that had been giving me so much concern since the doctor had given the okay for my afternoon out. The truth was that a vasectomy might have been a walk in the park compared to what 'endoscope' actually did.

Whenever I had visited a doctor or a hospital prior to the accident I had always been concerned when I had been in the situation of being left in a room whilst the doctor disappeared into another. On this occasion I had been left, not on my own, but with five nurses in attendance. I wasn't stupid enough to think that they were there to get to know me better, so my pleasure at a change of scenery was replaced very quickly by fear.

The language barrier had proved once again to be not so much a barrier, but more of a brick wall. It had been impossible for anyone to explain successfully to me what to expect. None of my German friends had been present to translate, so I was to discover the meaning of 'endoscope' as the procedure ran its course. Myself and a large chunk of trepidation lay rigid on the bed awaiting part one of the impending fun.

My first instruction indicated by example was simply to open my mouth, which I didn't find too trying. The next part wasn't quite so easy. One of the nurses loomed over my mouth with what appeared to be transparent flex. It was actually fibre optic cable. Somebody had decided that it was time to remove the tube still protruding from my stomach, but before this could be done, it was necessary to see if the healing process was running its course and no further damage would be done by taking the tube away. Unfortunately for me, taking a quick peek wasn't nearly sufficient and an internal examination was required. The fibre optic camera would show the doctors what they wanted to see on a television monitor next door.

At the back of your throat is the very sensitive spot and any prolonged contact with this induces vomiting. This was the first part of my anatomy to greet Mr Camera! This highly uncomfortable state of affairs wasn't helped by the fact that I could clearly feel the camera winding its way slowly down. It all became too much. Before this experience whenever I had heard about someone suffering a panic attack I had always found it extremely difficult to believe that you could just lose control for seconds, even minutes, then return to normal as if nothing had happened. I was about to find out.

My mental state became more and more panicky as I felt the cable on my throat and in my stomach. Then, without warning, I began to struggle violently. Each nurse, who was obviously there in preparation for this, grabbed the first part of my anatomy they could lay their hands on. Unfortunately for one of the nurses it was too late, as I had already got a secure grip on a part of *her* anatomy when I first went into panic mode. The cable wound its way deeper and deeper until it finally reached its destination. I had felt the entire arduous journey and when it finally reached the wound I felt that too. All of the panic escaped from my body along with various unpleasant bodily fluids. A small puddle of blood and vomit was cleaned away before the return journey to the familiar set of walls could begin. I would be pleased to see them. The nurses in turn released their grip on my body. I was still again after the brief flurry of pandemonium. One nurse was having my fingers released from her body, along with my nails that had entered her flesh at the height of my panic.

On my eventual return one kindly nurse told me to rest. I thanked her and reassured her that I didn't have any intention of going for a walk or a quick game of squash; rest was most definitely at the forefront of my mind. Maybe the patient in the next bed would not have reacted quite so badly at the experience but for me it was without doubt the worst thing that I was forced to endure during my entire stay in hospital. The period of rest that followed was, to say the least, unpleasant. I thought that I could never forget the experience yet in truth, unlocking and releasing a lot of the dormant panic within may have helped my recovery. I had been lying for so long for most of the time with only myself for company wondering how and why. That experience at least allowed me the opportunity to scream, shout and express my feelings.

I had been lying quietly on my bed for two hours that felt like two weeks, when yet another doctor appeared at my bedside. My already sore stomach was prodded gently with his fingers, tempting me to prod his eye with my own fingers, before he finally stopped. The endoscopy that had been so traumatic for me had obviously proved worthwhile. The picture on the monitor must have been crystal clear, despite my thrashing about. It had told the specialists exactly what they wanted to know and exactly what I had hoped for – they had found no problems. I worked out that fact for myself as without warning, he simply grabbed the tube and yanked it clear in one swift and incredibly painful move. I thanked him verbally, seconds after my fist had missed him by half an inch, and then collapsed and tried to recover. I was still quivering like a small child when I must have dozed off as the next I knew, it was morning.

The usual slops arrived under the cunning guise of breakfast. I missed the banquet yet again and chose to wash instead. The humiliating routine of sitting in full view of the rest of the ward and washing every nook and cranny of my body with a pathetic little square of cloth was made even more embarrassing by the nurse who had turned to that profession after failing as a shot-putter, keeping a beady eye on those nooks and crannies to make sure each was cleaned adequately. If she felt that was not the case, a large hand would grab the flannel and do the job for me. It was obvious that one of the side effects of being in a coma was that in my case pride had grown wings and buggered off back to England for a cup of tea and a cigarette!

I returned to my bed to prepare myself for yet another mind-numbingly boring day of just lying around thinking that under no circumstances could my life become any worse or any more embarrassing. Remember those slaps in the face? It had been a while but they were back.

The early part of the day turned out to be quite eventful. My parents called, as did Lucy and a brother. Tie these in with a visit from Christian and I almost felt wanted. My euphoria was unfortunately about to grow those wings and join pride back home in England.

Every day since I had been conscious, at approximately midday a doctor would arrive and quiz everyone in turn about the previous day. This would take a little longer with me due to the language barrier. On the first day this happened I was aware of being questioned about what I'd eaten, if I'd taken the medication left for me and finally, the last thing I was expecting anyone to ask – 'Have you shit yesterday?'

As the blood drained from my face he asked if this was fully understood by me. 'Shit, this is good, yes?'

I was quick to assure my student of the English language that I was fully aware of the meaning of his question and that in future the word 'shit' would be fine! A chuckle followed my reply, possibly an attempt to lighten the mood before his next duty. I began to worry about my safety, with the thought of perverse and highly questionable sexual activities springing to my disturbed mind, when, all of a sudden and without warning, a small plastic spatula-like object appeared from his pocket. At that time I was acutely aware of just how ill and helpless I was, but if I was going to pass on, I didn't want it to be at the hands of a sweaty German doctor with a perverse smile on his face!

The interrogation came to an abrupt halt, finishing with a word that I knew all too well. I was still desperately trying to convince anybody who would listen that I was about to vanish for one of the doctor's precious 'shits', when the word 'enema' hit me like a poisoned arrow. The lack of privacy that half of Leipzig had displayed back on that man-made beach, that was a novelty to all the Brits, was about to come back and haunt me as I was about to endure, without a doubt, the most embarrassing moments of my life. A full description of the episode is not required, except to say the Germans had obviously decided to have a joke at my expense.

Into the ward brandishing a length of garden hose and what appeared to be a bottle of bathroom cleanser walked the two most attractive nurses in the entire hospital, who would perform the duty. In horror and disbelief, I lay perfectly still throughout the ordeal without a shred of privacy. All of my fellow patients could watch my shame and turn away from me if I caught their eye, asking just how they would feel had the roles been reversed. To complete the humiliation when the unpleasant task was over, I was told to sit on a commode bang in the middle of the ward for all to see and try to ignore the laughter. A naked, white, underweight Englishman sitting on a toilet for all to see must have been an amusing sight to behold – if you have a warped sense of humour.

At the time I remember thinking how cruel the observers were being but with hindsight the episode does indeed seem mildly amusing. Fortunately for me at that point, my pride rose off its comfy seat back in England and returned to me in record time. Immediately, a curse was directed at the two nurses who did not look quite so attractive wearing pink plastic gloves, and I made my escape and headed off to the privacy of a proper toilet where I was to stay until the search party eventually found me and led me back to my bed. As I closed my eyes, I dwelt on the events of the previous hour and realised how wrong I had been earlier in the day when I had assumed that my life couldn't possibly get any worse. Surely, now I had reached that point?

I had been lying in my bed hiding from my shame for an hour when the next in the line of doctors and specialists wanting to see me, arrived. Had I been wrong again? Was life to become even worse after that doctor had done his job? Things began to look as if they were veering even further toward the bleak side when the doctor removed my bedsheet without warning, exposing every part of my anatomy that the other patients hadn't already seen on show. Events then appeared to bypass 'bleak' completely and head off into 'suicidal' as I observed the doctor slowly and deliberately applying a sinister looking jelly to the index finger of his right hand. I remember looking at him as his hand hovered over my person and I swear I saw a glint in his eye. My mind was racing as I tried desperately to remember every word of the German language that I knew and arrange them into a sentence that would roughly translate as, 'Just pass me a gun now.'

His eyes then turned to the open wound where the tube that he had ruthlessly removed the day before was staring at him angrily. His jelly-covered finger then revealed its purpose as, again without warning, he forcefully jabbed it directly into the wound. The jelly was obviously a healing solution, as at last the pain of my final tour in Germany came to an end.

'You can count the days until you go home now,' was the doctor's statement and the news that I had been long awaiting, yet still had a great deal of difficulty believing.

Ten minutes had passed since the tremendous news, when, with immaculate timing, Christian strolled into the ward and failed to get a word in edgeways as I waffled endlessly about my imminent departure. Christian decided to leave me in the ward and attempt to discover when the hospital would be discharging me. He left me still excitedly discussing my leaving with patients who couldn't even understand me. After Christian had discovered when I was going home he immediately informed my parents of the good news.

Ten days, just ten long days to go. My wounds had healed but, more importantly, the specialists were confident that I would be able to undertake the flight with no danger to my head. My parents immediately made all arrangements to come out to fetch me home. The flights were booked and the telephone bills began to mount up as did my excitement at the prospect of what felt like escape. A long night of sound sleep came to an end and I was to lie awake for an hour simply thinking of the pleasure to come. My naiveté towards the situation led me to believe that I had finished with hospitals for good and that I would be returning straight home. Unfortunately not, but I was going back to where the people understood me.

Then my train of thought was interrupted as the ward door swung open and Jim, my friend of twenty years walked in. 'Jesus Christ, how on earth did you get here?' I asked.

'I flew, you stupid bastard!' he replied and for the first time in eight weeks I laughed, loudly.

*

Conversation was an alien word to me since the coma. A good friend telling me what I had missed was exactly what I needed before returning home in readiness for the im- mense amount of talking I was going to have to do then. I am almost positive that had I at any time during the early part of being hospitalised been surrounded by more than two people who spoke English, I may well have fallen into total panic.

I had become used to prolonged company again by the time my mate began launching in to all the horror stories surrounding events back home which I had missed.

Numerous tales of relationships ending, drunken Christmas parties and drunken family arguments stirred up memories of a normal festive season back in England. Suddenly I was not all that upset at missing out on the 'fun'. The conversation had made me feel so much better. It was certainly true that my recovery would have been accelerated had I been able to connect with my surroundings, either physically or verbally in the early days of my stay on a regular basis. There was no doubt in my mind now that that was the case, but unfortunately it had been impossible. I just hadn't thought through the options properly before deciding it, as Germany was as good a place as any to leap head first down a stairwell.

My much appreciated visitor soon began to see and hear the effects of the blow to my head. Although I knew he was with me, where I was and why I was there, most of the thoughts in my mind were utterly nonsensical. Once one of those thoughts entered my head, it would have extreme difficulty leaving it again. I would refuse to believe Jim's explanations of the rubbish that I was spouting, sit back and wait for sanity to return.

Jim's two-day visit passed by quickly with me becoming obsessed with time. I would repeatedly ask him what the time was with the most common reply being, 'Two minutes after you last asked.' During my time in the hospital in a bedridden state, I had never once been able to see a clock or a watch. That was obviously no great loss when I was comatose and even immediately after awaking, when I didn't even know what a clock was. Now that I had rediscovered the concept of time, it became the most important thing in my life. Fortunately, soon after the departure of my friend and his wrist watch I discovered a clock hanging on the wall of the corridor outside the ward. I was by then spending a great deal of time simply wandering back and forth to witness time passing incredibly slowly. It was most definitely a good thing that there had been no clock in the ward itself as I would have been staring at the hands all day long and eventually have driven myself completely mad. Was that the reason for there being no way of telling the time? In hindsight it makes perfect sense.

I was now alone again, yet with a permanent smile on my face due to my impending departure. Six days to go and counting. The days really couldn't go quick enough, and they didn't.

Yet another side effect of my brain injury was the incredible tiredness that overpowered me at times. That fact was adding to my frustration at being in Germany. I would decide to go to sleep knowing that when I awoke another day had passed and that I was closer to going home. Unfortunately this would not be true. I would sleep for what felt like an extremely long and relaxing night, yet in actual fact it would transpire that I had only been asleep for an hour, maybe two if I was lucky.

It's Monday morning and you are due to return home after nine weeks in a foreign hospital in four days' time. You have the necessary four minutes of sleep that you need to get you through the days and are lying awaiting the reunion, the hugs, the kisses and the sheer thrill of going home, when a nurse appears carrying a telephone saying, 'It's for you.'

One of your brothers is on the other end of the line and you discuss how much you are looking forward to everything. When asked what you are doing at that precise moment in time, you reply, 'Waiting for Mum and Dad to arrive so that I can leave.'

As tactfully as possible you are then told, 'I don't know how to tell you this, mate, but they won't be there for another three days.' Upon learning that you haven't actually had four nights' sleep at all but only maybe one and three short naps you become so frustrated that you find yourself lying alone and crying. You don't even sit up to consider the fact that you are a grown man, crying. I was literally sat alone, crying because, to be perfectly honest, I personally couldn't give a shit what anybody who saw me thought. I would eventually pull myself together and realise that I hadn't looked at the clock for the infamous two minutes and return to my bed feeling slightly better.

Another morning arrived and yet another breakfast consisting of two mouthfuls before I discarded the rest. During my stay I had received such a fantastic array of meals that I had lost two stone in weight. It was all probably very edible and could quite easily have been very tasty indeed. Hospitals, as we all know only too well, have a stigma attached to them regarding the food. Everyone seems to think that it's the next step down from a meal on British Railways. When you are in the state I found myself in, you believe all the stories one hundred per cent. Your mind doesn't work properly. It is unable to understand the concept of humour and rumours that are blown out of all proportion. Tying these two factors together meant that I wasn't prepared to eat anything at all. I did, though, on occasion get to the point where I simply had to eat something, otherwise this wouldn't be me currently writing this saga.

Another day passed, during which the phone calls started to arrive again. Lucy called first. She now sounded as if she could not wait for me to return and a long call full of love and kisses made me pine all the more for home. I was now beginning to fully understand what was going on and was appreciating the calls from Lucy in particular rather than just being pleased to hear the voice of an English friend. No sooner had the telephone been returned, than it reappeared. Romy was on the line bidding farewell as I was to be leaving Leipzig before she would be able to visit again. A friendly chat with Romy soon made it clear to me that other parts of my body were coming back to life again and we said our goodbyes with me promising never to lose touch in order to thank her for her kindness and to hopefully repay it one day as good friends.

The day prior to my leaving Leipzig began with a visit from Christian. He would also be leaving Leipzig later that day so it was probably the last time I would ever see him. I certainly wasn't expecting to return to Germany myself and I didn't think that I would be seeing him in England. I didn't appreciate it at the time but sitting next to me was a man who six months earlier I hadn't even met, happily chatting away and handing over the keys to his flat to enable my parents to have a place to sleep on their arrival. He was doing absolutely everything in his power to make the whole experience as painless for me and my family as possible. I later learned that his flat had been used as a hotel for my parents on two occasions, my brother had stayed there almost every day he had spent in the country, along with Lucy twice, George and also a couple of friends from England who visited, which I don't remember.

People have said to me since, 'Well, I would have done the same thing.' But would they? Think about it: some ten foreign, complete strangers using your home as living quarters, handing them the keys when you can't be there yourself and then trusting them to get them back to you. You would probably just point them in the direction of the cheapest hotel. Luckily, not so for us. After a traditional hearty handshake, Christian left with one final parting gift. He would attempt to arrange transport to get us to the airport the following day. I thanked him profusely one more time and off he went with emotional goodbyes ringing in our ears.

A doctor arrived at midday and launched into his final volley of questions. I almost cried when for the very last time I heard those immortal words, 'Have you shit yesterday?' Since that unfortunate and well-documented day, I had devised a cunning plan that was to shield me from further humiliation until I left. I simply answered a stern 'Yes' to every question that was thrown at me. My plan seemed to work and nothing even remotely resembling a hose and a bottle of bathroom cleaner came anywhere near my body again.

With twenty-four hours to go until my departure, my bed was actually starting to feel comfortable. For the first time in what was by then nine weeks, I sat and relaxed. Christian had left me with an English newspaper that he had specially bought for me at the train station. I attempted to read it but it was impossible. I couldn't concentrate on anything at all, with my thoughts firmly locked on home. It was at that moment I decided that the whole hospital and not just the medics I had seen was having one big joke at my expense.

The patient in the bed next to me who I hadn't paid any attention to all the time I had been there, and vice versa, had a visitor who left with him a small portable television set. That didn't unduly bother me. My limited grasp of the German language meant that I would be reduced to simply looking at the pictures and failing to follow any storyline that might exist. Therefore, sport was the only thing worth watching as I didn't need a running commentary. Being a big fan of sport myself, watching anything from the sporting world would have cheered me and given me something to concentrate on. My fellow patient with immaculate timing turned on his set and immediately tuned it into the sports channel. He kindly asked me it I wanted to watch and placed it so we could both see the pictures. Nine long weeks and the television finally arrived, just a little too late, I watched what was without a doubt the most tedious game of tennis I had ever seen, but for some reason it gripped me entirely. I can remember every point and every bad line call. By coincidence, the game in question was a Davis Cup encounter featuring Germany. I sat quietly cheering for the opposition only to be disappointed.

Lucy made her final phone call to me in Germany. I was convinced that I would be going home direct from the airport in England and bypassing any hospitals. Although I then had a more realistic understanding of what had occurred, I was still to fully take in the seriousness of my condition. I was under the impression that I could walk out of the hospital, fly home to England without so much as a yawn and be driven home where I would celebrate my homecoming in the pub with everyone I knew!

After a fond farewell from Lucy there was only one night of sleep before my parents' arrival. There followed a night that reminded me of being six and attempting to sleep on Christmas Eve. I nodded off for an hour here and there, but didn't have what could be described as a good solid night of sleep. At long last one of the numerous short naps came to an end and signalled morning.

It was 6 a.m. and I had no idea at all what time my parents would be arriving, despite the fact that I had been told the day before. After a knock on the head it is very common for the short-term memory to become distorted. I was certainly having that particular problem myself. I could remember things that happened ten years ago as if they had happened the previous day. Two minutes ago was... two minutes ago was... two minutes ago was occasionally a problem for me to recall – very frustrating. I would put down the telephone and sometimes forget that anyone had called. That didn't bother me at all at the time. It was only later after my return home that people would tell me what they had said and I could recall nothing. I couldn't even remember the smallest parts of our conversations and nothing reminded me of them. A total void. Those phone calls did punctuate the loneliness that I felt but unfortunately they would only cheer me while they lasted as before long I would forget them again. Occasionally, one call would stick in my mind and my brain had become very choosy about what it would allow me to recall at a later date.

I craved attention from the people I knew well, but when it arrived, had little interest. Often Christian would arrive and more than once a two-minute conversation would end with me feigning tiredness and he would leave again. It was perhaps unnecessary to fake the tiredness as had I waited for another minute I would more than likely have been exhausted anyway but I was dishonest all the same.

The seconds were ticking by at the rate of one every hour, a phenomenon caused by my obsession with the clock outside the ward. Eventually a nurse wandered by with her trolley of poisons which she preferred to call 'dinner'. I was virtually dragged from my chair away from the clock hanging on the wall and another plate of un-cooked meat was duly ignored. For the first time during my stay in the hospital, I had a believable excuse. My parents were arriving later that day and with them they would be bringing real, edible food. The German habit of dishing up food that looked, felt, tasted and smelt as if it had been placed in direct sunlight for ten minutes to cook it meant that anything placed in front of me that I classed as edible would be consumed with vigour. I was carrying with me a hunger that had appeared shortly after the coma but no amount of German hospital food could tempt me into stemming it. The need for decent food had long since wiped out my cravings for a cigarette. For someone who had been getting through somewhere in the region of thirty a day, the lack of nicotine also added to making the day that much longer. As most smokers will tell you, the habit is just that – a habit, merely something to do. Take it away and for a brief spell you are lost.

Another visit to see my best friend Mr Clock told me that it was midday and still my parents hadn't arrived. Each of the nurses had said their farewells at the end of their shifts. One of the lovely ladies even told me her address and asked me to keep in touch with a glint in her eye. Foolishly I made no attempt to make a note of this. She had previously been extremely friendly and made my days just a little more cheerful. She had also made a point of vanishing into the background whenever Lucy had visited, so I was informed later. If only I knew then what I know now. It didn't even cross my mind that anyone wanted to be nice to me rather than just treating me. I said goodbye to her and then realised that the last time anybody had found me devastatingly attractive was a gentleman by the name of Helmut who had accosted me at 3 a.m. at Frankfurt train station, nine months previously.

I wasn't unduly bothered about it as I had Lucy waiting at home, terribly concerned and looking forward to seeing me in a way that I had rarely been aware of, if at all. Every time I had returned home during my stay in Germany, it had seemed to be a case of going through the motions as opposed to her being genuinely pleased to see me. Maybe a combination of having a serious accident and no longer owing her any money brought about false feelings of love on her side of the relationship. There was a chance, like flipping a coin. Nobody could tell how long the coin would be in the air, but when it finally came down it would be heads – love, tails – goodbye! The near future, however, was destined to be the period of time that the coin would spend spinning in the air and dropping to the ground slowly. The outcome was a mystery to everyone.

I was to unwittingly make the whole situation more complicated due to my lack of mental stability. I still couldn't remember anything about the accident or the subsequent treatment in the first month following it. My brain seem confused by missing that small part of my life and to make up for the loss, my mind replaced the void with facts that weren't even true but which I believed entirely. I had made them all up by myself and as much as I knew what my own name was, those thoughts were just as certain to me. There was one particular untruth that was destined to make my whole state of mind much more uncertain in the future weeks. It wouldn't reveal itself until my parents arrived and we had got the tearful reunions out of the way. Speaking of which, by 2 p.m. I was getting decidedly worried.

I had been sitting and mulling over the events of the nine weeks for the whole of the day since 6 a.m., stopping only for one or two short sleeps, when after my afternoon cup of coffee a nurse arrived. She stood perfectly still in the doorway and made no attempt to advance into the ward. I was beginning to think just how strange her behaviour was when her arm rose from her side and she began to beckon me with a single finger, whilst smiling widely. I slowly got up and prepared myself for yet another injection or test of some kind. I found it unusual that I was being led from the ward for that purpose, as everything previously had taken place with me prone on my bed. The reason finally became very clear as I left the ward. I made my way slowly into the corridor to be greeted by very shocked and emotional parents. The last time they had seen me, it had been physically impossible for me to get out of a bed, let alone walk unaided down a corridor.

Prolonged and tearful greetings were joined by a copious amount of hugging from my very relieved mother and the long discussions began. It was first pointed out to me that we would actually be returning home in two days' time in order to allow my parents the opportunity to visit the people who had helped to make their previous stays a little less stressful. That was not a problem to me; learning that I was being transported to yet another hospital back in my home town was a little more disturbing. I had no desire to go anywhere other than my home. The last thing I needed was to be escaping from nine weeks in a German hospital only to be taken to one in England.

However, that bad news headed quickly for the back of my mind when food started to appear from my father's travel bag. The two stone in weight that I had shed was still out there somewhere and so I set about trying to retrieve it. Meanwhile my still-numb mother was reduced to just looking at me in a kind of 'you could be dead' way – a fact that hadn't even crossed my mind at the time.

All the time I was firing questions at both of them about everyone at home who I hadn't seen for weeks, at least so I thought. Lucy's name inevitably wasn't long in cropping up and at that point in the conversation my confusion kicked in. For no reason at all I had become convinced that myself and Lucy were getting engaged during the Christmas break that I had so spectacularly missed. This of course wasn't true – it hadn't even been discussed. I didn't know that at the time though. It all seemed very real to me and so I naturally assumed that Lucy was looking forward to my return for that reason also. My parents were obviously unaware of that joyous news, but gave their congratulations anyway whilst asking why nothing had been mentioned before then.

My parents took quite some time to get past the 'thank God he's still alive' stage and I never got past the stage of being tremendously excited simply to have English-speaking visitors with me all day. My father's eventual announcement that the two of them would be departing for an hour to find somewhere they could eat was met by a scowl and pleas for them not to leave. That was a show of affection rarely seen and only abject loneliness was causing it on that occasion. For my sake and mainly because of the pleas, my parents threw a cheeseburger down their throats and returned quickly. During their brief trip away I had eaten the tasty sandwiches that they had brought with them and stuck two fingers up to the unsuspecting nurse who had arrived with a meal.

After a further two hours of talking, the journey started to take its toll on Mum and Dad. The excitement and the conversation had started to make me yawn as well. After nine weeks in the hospital doing nothing more than looking around the ward, suddenly having two permanent visitors meant that I had to do an awful lot of thinking. This was something my mind had not been used to for quite some time. If an athlete fails to train for a period of time, his body will soon not be as fit as it once was. That was exactly what had happened to my brain throughout the time I had been comatose. Overdosing on company and conversation was making me tire even quicker, not just yawning a little earlier than I normally would either. I was totally exhausted. This problem was to last for a lot longer than the duration of my parents' visit.

I was almost pleased to wave goodbye that evening as they left to visit Claudia, the nurse from the intensive care unit who had opened up her home to them in that first weekend of total panic. Claudia had apparently visited me after my return to consciousness and my brother had had the pleasure of attempting to get me to make sense. I had, so I am told, been just a little rude to her as I had no idea at all who the strange woman asking me questions was. Even when told of what she had done for my parents, I had failed to be at all interested, told her to piss off and got back to talking rubbish. At that time I wasn't exactly the most pleasant man on earth to spend time with. I was unable to slip out of the foul-mouthed builder persona although then I wasn't sure whether I was a foul-mouthed builder, a farmer or perhaps even a hairdresser!

Chapter Eight

Home at Last

The first good night's sleep that I could remember having in the hospital positively raced by and I was there. The day had finally arrived. I was going home. Well, going to an English hospital anyway. That would have to do for the time being. Before I was able to relive my recurring dream of walking out of the hospital, all of my belongings had to be packed. I wasn't even aware that I had any belongings in the hospital, but upon opening the small cupboard next to my bed I discovered a wealth of magazines brought by various visitors. A cassette recorder with headphones that I could vaguely recall abandoning as soon as I had turned it on, was there also. I remember trying to listen to it once and the noise being more infuriating than enjoyable because of my extreme sensitivity to, well, everything! To one side of the cupboard, standing on a shelf, was a small stack of get well soon cards addressed to me. I could vaguely remember the cassette recorder but that was the first I had known about any cards. A quick scan through revealed concern for me from both countries. At some point during my stay I had received cards from parents, brothers, aunts, uncles, friends and other people who had simply heard the news and wanted to let me know they were thinking about me, and I remembered not one of them.

In my nine weeks' stay everything that Christian had arranged had been very much appreciated. Unfortunately, his last effort to arrange transport to take us to the airport hadn't come to fruition and a taxi was promptly booked. There was just enough time to have one last cup of hospital coffee in order to remember just how atrocious it actually was. With perfect timing, as the three of us finished our drinks, one of the nurses informed us that a taxi was waiting outside. I stood bolt upright as quickly as my sore back allowed and then it became clear to me why a wheelchair had entered the ward with my parents. I wanted more than anything to be able to walk out of the hospital, but a combination of my own sense and my parents' insistence meant the wheelchair was the sensible option eventually chosen. As we made our way out of the ward and through the maze of corridors, I said my farewells to the nurses we passed and after a two-minute journey the exit was in front of me. This door was a common sight for my parents, but it was obviously the very first time that I had seen any of the hospital other than the intensive care unit, the ward I was eventually moved to, and of course the dreaded endoscope chamber. However, I was in no mood for sightseeing; I just wanted to get home. We left the building and in no time I had moved from the wheelchair into the waiting taxi. My parents climbed in after me and we finally left the grounds. I felt that the whole painful experience had at last come to an end. I didn't expect to see Germany again and intended to forget all about the country. Never did a twenty-minute drive seem to last as long as that one to the airport.

The cafeteria at Leipzig airport that I ignored on my numerous excursions through the building in the preceding months was now gripping my attention with an all-consuming force. Each and every sandwich on view looked to me like a three-course meal and it wasn't long before the three of us had a delicious sandwich and a much better cup of coffee in front of us. Even though I was famished to the extent of drooling over the crumbs, one sandwich was all I could eat as my stomach had shrunk to the size of a walnut. I was determined to put that right on my arrival back home by putting my taste buds through some serious punishment. The practice run at the airport prepared me superbly. Fed, watered and content, the call came to board our flight right on time.

It was then for the first time in my life that I began to understand the problems faced every day by wheelchair-bound people. I was fortunate enough to be able to discard mine the next day, but briefly saw for myself how mind-numbingly frustrating life can be when you are confined to one of those damned chairs. Almost every aspect of every-day living that able-bodied people take for granted becomes a task, and an arduous one at that. A good idea would be for every able-bodied person to spend just one day of their lives experiencing how it feels to be in a wheelchair. Although just one day is a drop in the ocean of disability, it may well help dispel the ignorance that most of us have of one of the things in life we are certain will never happen to ourselves. My instinct to climb out of the chair and run across the tarmac to the waiting aircraft had to be curbed as I was wheeled to the steps where two of the airline staff were standing. I was deftly lifted out of my temporary mode of transport and carried on to the plane where I was placed into the comfortable seat reserved for me with a parent sat on either side.

The moment the engines began to whine was the first time that my thoughts had turned to Lucy that day. Waiting for me at home along with her were all the friends and family I so looked forward to seeing. My excitement was still being tempered, though, by the knowledge of yet another hospital bed being the first thing waiting for me on my arrival back in my home town. There was just the small matter of the flight to go through first.

I was now fully aware of everything that had happened to me, almost entirely from listening to others rather than from what my own mind could drag out of the vacuum that was my memory. I had woken one day in a foreign hospital, wondering why I was there and spent the rest of my time trying to work out that little conundrum. I hadn't dwelt on how serious my injuries were, as I hadn't been aware of most of them. When I had at last been able to understand what people were saying to me, being told I had a broken skull and brain damage had the same impact on me as being told I had broken a finger!

The thought of flying so soon afterwards, only worries me now. At the time I certainly wasn't thinking about the dangers of air pressure. I was more worried about the slightly uneasy stomach that our sandwich at the airport had been kind enough to leave me with. The uneasy feeling turned to outright nausea as the plane departed from terra firma and began to ascend into the afternoon sky. Although I had flown to Germany on every visit since the initial ferry trip, I had yet to shake off my dislike of the pastime. I don't have a phobia; I just simply do not like it. The take-off being over and done with was a huge relief until I remembered that the flight to London wasn't direct. After a short stop at Hanover, the whole exercise would be repeated. Anything that got in the way of my homecoming annoyed the hell out of me. I wasn't just looking forward to being there, I felt that I needed to be there to speed up my recovery.

The short flight ended and we landed at Hanover. I had done the trip more than once with Terry and remembered the need to leave the aircraft and pass through passport control before departing again for London. Fortunately the airline had taken into account the fact that I was in a wheelchair and avoided further delays by allowing myself and my parents to stay on the plane. The stop lasted an hour that felt like a day and then the rest of the passengers began to board again. Fingers were clenched and teeth were gritted as the engines started to whine again, sounding almost bored with the monotony of the day. I had some sympathy as the plane rose off the ground along with everything in it, apart from my stomach and its contents, for what was the second time in as many hours. That was it! The next time my feet touched the ground it would be on English soil.

Just as my stomach had returned to my body and got to grips with the 'lovely' in-flight meal, the plane once more began slowly to descend. The much anticipated and yearned-for homecoming was at long, long last nearly upon me. The few minutes that it took the aircraft to fall gracefully out of the sky passed by and a tell-tale thud announced the rubber hitting the tarmac. My own private 'whoop' rang out loud inside my head. On leaving the plane it was only the fact that I was in the wheelchair that prevented me from going down on my knees and kissing the ground, Pope-style again. It was such an immense relief to be home. I immediately felt an awful lot of the worry, the tension and, most importantly, the loneliness, lift off my shoulders.

I had been convinced on the day before we left Leipzig that I would be able to travel all the way home comfortably without tiring at all. Fortunately my parents were blessed with the sanity that I was still sadly lacking. Close friends lived only a short drive from the airport and on earlier visits made by my parents they had provided some much needed hospitality. Our own journey home on that occasion was to be broken by a sizeable home-cooked meal, conversation and what I was looking forward to the most – a comfortable bed that our friends would provide.

At the airport there was much hugging and handshaking, followed by the short journey from Heathrow to Bracknell. Twenty-four hours earlier I had been talking to my parents, which in itself felt strange. Two English people in close proximity to me was an event that I couldn't remember since the day before my plummet down the stairwell. After my arrival home I was then surrounded by four people who wanted to talk to me not just for medical reasons and possessing a far greater vocabulary than, 'Have you shit yesterday?' I was almost overwhelmed but excitement staved off this threat.

Things got better when we arrived at the home of our friends when a television set was turned on, surrounding me with an almost endless supply of chat that I could understand. It was superb. I don't think I have ever felt so happy and relaxed as I did that evening. The happiness turned to euphoria when the food arrived and my stomach began to feel very spoilt indeed.

As the hours ticked by I failed to become at all fatigued. I was prepared to sit and talk all night and if my companions failed to last the pace, I would simply sit and watch the television, consumed with interest. Eventually however, the need for sleep did overwhelm me and a comfortable mattress beckoned me. It did not seem as if I would be able to sleep at all as I lay there in unfamiliar surroundings. The bed didn't have bars lifted around the sides to stop me from climbing out unannounced as the one in hospital had. The strange feeling can't have lasted for long, though, as breakfast was soon upon me. I had obviously achieved an unbroken night of sleep as over breakfast I was informed of the visits made into my room simply to check all was well. I had no memory of anything beyond climbing on to the mattress.

It isn't often that your emotions turn full circle between falling asleep and waking the next morning, but this was the case for me. I realised when I woke up that I would soon be confined to a hospital yet again. After all it was only a day since I had happily walked out of the German hospital, revelling in the pleasure of doing something more than just having the day broken up by a friendly nurse brandishing a syringe! The prospect of yet more syringes loomed at the next hospital but it would be mostly down to me how long I would have to stay there. I could either sit around feeling sorry for myself all day, letting all my concerned relatives and friends pamper me, or get off my backside and try to get back to normal.

It does take a little time to stop feeling sorry for yourself; that's inevitable. However, I didn't feel even the smallest twinge of bitterness towards anything or anyone else about the accident. People were constantly asking me if I had a 'Why me?' attitude towards what happened that day. To be totally honest, it hadn't even crossed my mind that I was unlucky to be injured in the way that I was. When I arrived back in England, I still had no recollection of what happened and was still not fully aware of the injuries I had to contend with. Consequently at this stage I didn't really have much to be bitter or upset about. It remained to be seen whether any of these feelings would manifest themselves in my mind in the days to come.

As the luggage was being loaded into our car, my eagerness to see everyone was tempered by the knowledge that I would soon be back in hospital and the first in a very long line of sighs filled the morning air. We thanked our friends for everything and disappeared on to the motorway nearby. I can clearly remember every single metre of that journey which seemed to me to be passing by at a frightening pace. My parents told me months after that trip that my mood was such that my mother was convinced that there was every chance I would fling open a door and leap out. However, although I was badly injured and quite unwell, I wasn't that stupid. The hundred and eighty mile journey went by at a steady sixty sighs an hour and by mid-afternoon my next temporary home stood gleaming hygienically before me. It wasn't what you could call a homey sight and I certainly wasn't at all happy to be there.

On entering the building I couldn't help seeing every detail of the hospital ward in Germany that I'd spent so much time staring at. Every medical instrument was still crystal clear in my mind, along with how many tiles were on the floor, the scratches on the paintwork and other tedious yet time-consuming facts. The lack of things to occupy my mind had led me through an assortment of primary school pastimes in order to do just that, pass time. I knew which of my friends had the highest telephone number if all the digits were added together and tried to work out who had the highest value name if the letters in their name had a numerical value. After taking six days to work out the first name and finding that it was wrong anyway, I gave up on that one due to my lack of brain power.

On being shown around the ward in England, I could see all of the tedium of the last nine weeks would not be repeated. Edible food, a comfortable bed, a television, nurses who I could understand and unlimited visiting hours softened the blow. Yet it still only took two minutes for me to launch somewhat aggressively into my 'I want to go home' routine. Much work had been done on my behalf to enable me to be transferred to the hospital. I could not be discharged from hospital in Germany until a suitable rehabilitation clinic had been found for my continued treatment. The nurses had been told what to expect, but had not been made aware of the fact that I was going to act like a spoilt child, as good as threatening to scream if I was not allowed to go home. I was left at my bed with my parents persuading me that I had to go along with what was happening. The more I made things difficult the longer I would have to stay in hospital. I began to figure this out for myself after about an hour.

The first English doctor to see me arrived five minutes after I'd settled in to give me the usual brief examination, blood pressure, reflexes etc. After this she told me of the immediate plans to assess my condition by seeing various consultants. Home was something that didn't enter the equation until this was done. The first person to see me after that was the physiotherapist whose job it seemed to me was to put my body into different awkward positions to see just how mobile I was and to note any effects of my injuries that could not be seen by sitting and talking, cracked vertebrae in particular.

Next to come was an occupational therapist. Her job was to see whether I could successfully and confidently achieve everyday tasks that before the accident had been everyday tasks. Having an attractive nurse watching me washing and dressing, made me wonder initially if this was necessary or if the nurse was just kinky! However this thought soon disappeared when a look in a mirror revealed an under-nourished individual who clearly hadn't exercised for weeks.

The neuropsychologist would see me after I'd settled in and begun to appreciate that I was back home. Neuropsychologist is a name that made me think of straitjackets and secure rooms with bouncy walls. I would mull over these thoughts in the days to come as I awaited my discharge.

My bed in the ward was only a few feet from a sizeable window which gave a clear sighting of anyone or anything entering the grounds. When Lucy arrived on that first day though, I had no idea, as her new car threw me off the scent. She strode in with a cheery smile on her face, almost as wide as mine, but not quite. Vigorous hugging and a peck on the cheek made everything all right and I hadn't been that happy ever. I was home, and my girl was next to me. I felt like writing a country and western song! It looked like things were improving. After an afternoon in the clinic, any thoughts of feeling sorry for myself had been well and truly knocked out of me. Compared to virtually all of my fellow patients in the clinic I must have seemed a perfectly fit visitor who was there to see someone else. I was surrounded by people who couldn't walk, couldn't live on their own, couldn't breathe without help and were destined to spend the rest of their lives in either that clinic or a similar place that could tend to their needs. The wheelchair that had been used to return me home in had by then been taken away and as I was unsteadily walking around the clinic, I couldn't help being attacked by pangs of guilt. Any feelings of 'Why me' were nudged aside before they had time to develop and a feeling of good fortune took their place. I felt almost privileged to be able to walk, but at that time I was still unable to see that in actual fact I was lucky to be just breathing.

The first meal to face me since my arrival at the clinic was placed in front of me after two hours of being so incredibly pleased to see Lucy that no thoughts of food had entered my mind. At long last I was in a hospital where, as it became apparent when the meal arrived, the food was most definitely edible. Unlike in Germany, the meat was cooked. That small point in itself was a pleasant change for me after nine months of attempting to eat the famous German delicacy that is Wurst. To a lot of people, most of them Teutonic, I am sure Wurst is simply delicious, yet to me it is the most revolting and foul-smelling culinary 'delight' ever to be placed on a plate and offered to an unsuspecting diner! It is plain to see that the discovery of Wurst in all its forms had come after one of their notoriously long drinking sessions, when sanity had long since vanished in a blur of alcohol.

I didn't take long to consume my dinner and it was quickly followed by a small selection from the array of goodies brought in by Lucy, along with a selection of Christmas presents that were an attempt to relive for me all the celebrations from two months previously that I had slept through. It didn't work; nothing ever could, or ever will.

It is an unusual sensation when you sit back and try to remember a part of your life, but nothing materialises. I can't even begin to imagine how it must feel when your mind returns to normality after months or even years in a coma. The frustration must be intense. Those feelings must become even more intense if, like me, the first weeks after regaining consciousness are also extremely unclear, adding to the period of memory loss.

As I sat excitedly talking to Lucy, a nurse interrupted us by telling me that I had received a phone call. That was the first time since the accident that I had been informed of a call as opposed to someone with no grasp of my language, simply holding the receiver aloft and pointing at it, then me.

'I told you it would be soon,' said my brother on the other end of the line, referring back to his soothing words as he left me in Germany for the last time. At that point in time, I had been convinced that there was no way that I would ever be returning home. Every visitor who disappeared back home made the feeling even stronger. Fortunately for me on that occasion, his words had been prophetic. Everyone who had come to see me in Germany or spoken to me over the telephone had obviously told me that I would be home soon. I knew that there was no truth in their assurances and that they were just attempting to pacify me. At long last, on the thousandth time of telling, my brother had got it right and wasted no time at all reminding me of the fact.

He would visit me that night with his wife to spend some time with me on our own turf and it would be fantastic to see him again. The mood on the visit could at last be jovial. It was at that point that I started to feel time hurtling by at a pace that was quite frightening. In the space of forty-eight hours I had gone from time seeming to pass at a snail's pace as I lay waiting for my departure from Germany, to the hours flying by as I became reacquainted with Lucy and my family.

I was basking in the glow that conversing in English was giving me. My parents were thrilled to have me back in England, Lucy was very excited that I was back within reach and a long list of family and friends were waiting to see me. All those pleasures still took a distant second place to my repeated requests to be discharged that were eventually directed at anyone remotely medical who happened to stray within talking distance of my bed. As it became apparent that I would have to stay at the unit for more than two hours, I resigned myself to that fact, thereby scrapping my master plan to pester everyone, particularly the staff, to such an extent that they would send me home just to shut me up.

My second edible meal in six hours arrived and was hurriedly consumed yet again. My body had scarcely time to digest the contents of the meal when my brother arrived in a similar way to Lucy, loaded down with crisps and chocolate and not surprisingly I found just a little more room in my already expanding stomach for just a bit more.

When late that evening two of my friends arrived, I had begun to tire from the endless hugging and handshaking. In actual fact, I was beginning to tire from everything. Fortunately for me, the unit I had been transferred to was very open and allowed visitors to stop for as long as they wanted. I wanted all of mine to stay and keep me company for ever. All the travelling and the culture shock got the better of me eventually though, and I was forced to ask my visitors to leave in order for me to get the sleep that all of a sudden I so desperately needed, despite the fact that I had been doing exactly that for most of the previous nine weeks.

After the departure of my visitors, I remained wide awake for an hour staring at the television thoroughly enjoying whatever it was I was watching. Then suddenly with no warning my body began to rebel against the massive intake of food that it was not used to and the next hour was spent staring at a toilet. I thought better of informing any of the staff of my sickness as I had no wish to jeopardise any chance of going home. Mercifully I must have fallen asleep shortly after my lavatorial adventures and woke eight hours later in a state of panic. I had opened my eyes and failed to recognise any of my surroundings. I finally remembered where I was and a broad grin replaced the furrowed brow.

Breakfast disappeared as quickly as it had arrived and I sat back waiting for the next influx of visitors. My eagerness was interrupted by yet another medical examination and a nurse with a list of questions regarding my general health. The answers I gave would give the specialists an idea of the therapy, if any, I would be needing in the weeks and months to follow. One of the first questions I was asked was how often I was suffering from headaches. 'Never,' was the reply. It was difficult for me to understand how I could break my skull, part of it embedding itself in my brain, and not suffer a single twinge in my head since I had come out of the coma. Long may it stay that way, I remember thinking.

As the specialists saw me one by one and my injuries were examined, it was becoming apparent that when I had been in a coma I had passed those three doors mentioned earlier. I had ignored the bad ones and chosen 'lucky bastard'. Still, there was plenty of time for that to change.

I was about to finish undergoing my first medical that day when Lucy arrived only eleven hours after leaving me the previous night. Yet more tremendously sickly foodstuffs were placed on my lap and despite my sickness of the night before I tucked in greedily. Uncooked German meat was by then an almost forgotten experience.

We had been chatting for only ten minutes when my second brother strolled in. It was apparently a pleasant change for him to see me happily welcoming him. The last time he had seen me I could have been on Mars. Another vast selection of Christmas gifts was opened and the pile of chocolate at the foot of my bed could have fed a small third-world country, which coincidentally was exactly what my stomach felt like.

I had just begun to tuck in when Jim who had visited me in Germany only a week previously greeted me. He had been my last overseas visitor and we carried on with the conversation that we had only half-finished when his appointment with an aeroplane brought it to an end. Although it hadn't been long since our last meeting, my memory needed reminding of what the conversation had been about.

Being home was making me feel a lot better but it didn't automatically mean that my injuries, physically and mentally, would right themselves. My memory was testament to this as I still remembered nothing regarding the accident and virtually all of my stay in the German hospital. A doctor informed me that that was a very common problem for victims of a head injury. This didn't help as I still couldn't figure out why I could remember people visiting, but drew a complete blank when attempting to recall conversations. Jim did eventually remind me of the conversation we had been having when he was forced to depart. I hadn't been in a good mood then and had spent the afternoon being extremely unpleasant to one of my fellow patients. Fortunately, he had had no idea that I was being unpleasant anyway due to the language barrier.

Our banter was interrupted by the arrival of another meal. I had now been in the clinic for twenty-four hours. During the whole time I had been constantly gorging on countless bars of chocolate and various other gifts brought by my friends and family. The only liquids to enter my body during the time had been very, very strong coffee that I hadn't been able to taste due to the abundance of sugar I had placed in each cup. After all of that extravagance I had vomited furiously during the night and now I was starting all over again. After all of that indulgence and despite the painful memories of my constant hunger in Germany, it had only taken a short space of time for me to realise on viewing the first meal of the day how truly awful hospital food actually is. There is something about looking at food that has been cooked five miles away that is distinctly off-putting. Rather than appear totally ignorant, I chose to eat one potato as a token gesture and then returned to the chocolate mountain at the side of my bed. It would not be long before the weight I had lost would return.

No sooner had my brother and friend left than Terry walked in. For the first time I was given a graphic description of the events of that fateful day, Terry being one of the first to see me lying at the foot of the stairwell, groaning loudly. Along with another of the English crew, he had come to the conclusion that I was having a sleep down there and the groans were nothing more than snores. The first sight of blood had forced the truth on to them and a little more urgency. An ambulance had been called and conversation centred on the stupidity of having no safety rails of any description surrounding the two-storey drop. Photos were taken by one of the lads and two medics set about the precarious task of getting me out of there without the aid of steps. The lack of knowledge of the extent of my injuries at that time meant that it had to be a very slow and gentle procedure and I feel that they made a superb job of it.

All the details of the accident being relayed to me didn't upset me at all. Already I was attempting to forget what had happened and concern myself more with what was coming in the weeks and months ahead. Although it is impossible to forget entirely what put you in the position you are in, you have to try and put it as far to the back of your mind as you can. Dwelling on it will be no help at all as you try to recover your fitness. As with anything negative that happens in your life, thinking about it for twenty-four hours a day will do nothing more than drag you down. Eventually you'll become bitter towards whatever or whoever caused the slump that you find yourself in. In the end it is impossible to concentrate your efforts on anything else.

I was aware of the possibility of falling into that downward spiral and I wasn't that pleased that Terry was sitting on my bed. He had been around at the time of the accident and knew what happened. Everyone else I had come into contact with could only speculate. He proceeded to chat happily about the events of that day, looking cheerful and immensely healthy. I don't know if Terry felt fortunate to be the visitor but he certainly was. It could have been any of the workers on the site, English or German who had gone down that well. Unfortunately, I had been the one who had grabbed the short straw over breakfast as we prepared for work that morning. I had, at that time, no desire at all to sit with Terry and swap tales of the months we had spent in Germany. I had to eventually make that fact clear and explain that I would be happier if he went home and left me to spend time with people who I hadn't lived and worked with for the six months before the accident.

The rest of that second day was spent relaxing with the visitors who had been kind enough to make the short journey to see me, and pestering even more nurses to put a good word in for me to the specialists who would eventually send me smiling all the way home. Almost two days of non-stop harassment had failed to sway the medical staff caring for me into sending me home. That didn't deter me as I planned to continue my campaign of terror during the time that I was to spend with the final member of the medical team to assess me, the neuropsychologist. Meanwhile, I could just sit and talk with my loved ones, while once again viewing the less fortunate patients around me, which in itself made me feel grateful to be me.

Some of the visitors who arrived on that second day included friends and members of the family whom I had completely forgotten about as it had been so long since I had seen them, yet who on hearing of my brief attempt at free fall had been extremely concerned for me. In Germany I had spent so much time by myself that the only thought in my head was wanting to see as many people as possible. On arriving home, however, even I was surprised and overwhelmed by the number of visitors who came to see me. It's only when you experience that side of the recovery process that you sit down and realise how bad the accident must have been, to have that many people concerned enough to be at your bedside within a day or so of your return. The worry and stress that everyone had gone through was in stark contrast to my own part in it all. I had spent the best part of ten weeks hardly aware of events and consequently didn't worry unduly. Only in the final couple of weeks did the severity of my situation become clearer to me and even then I spent most of it sound asleep.

The day ended with just myself and Lucy wishing each other a passionate goodnight after a friendly nurse, who had seen Lucy giving me a quick peck on the cheek, had rushed over, pulled the curtain around my bed and said, 'If you're going to do it, do it properly.'

This was a very different attitude from the cold and clinical atmosphere that I had left behind. I am sure most of the nurses were nice enough people but when you have a limited grasp of a language, every time you attempt to speak to somebody who is fluent in it, you will more often than not sound abrupt and without emotion. That was undoubtedly the case where my conversations with the medical staff in Germany was concerned. On top of that inconvenience, I had just spent time in a country where the people are renowned for being brash and abrupt anyhow.

After Lucy's emotional departure I made friends once again with the television before slipping into sleep. The rest would do me good in preparation for the following day, when I would be talking to the neuropsychologist. The thought of this was sounding a little daunting. How could I express my feelings to a total stranger when I was having great difficulty understanding them myself? I came to the conclusion that the best course of action would be to tell the man what I thought he would want to hear, which didn't necessarily have to be the truth. I would just do enough to get myself discharged and then think rationally when I was back at home, with my feet up, a cup of tea in one hand, a cigarette in the other and a purring cat sat on my lap. That night I kept waking up to rehearse my lines. I would only get one chance and I didn't want to make a mess of it – there was no telling how long I would have to stay if I did. I was fortunate enough to have all of my script fresh in my mind when I awoke in the morning to be greeted by a cheery smile and a hot cup of coffee. It would be my third day in the clinic and my immediate thoughts were that the scenery wasn't getting any better. Still, there was a chance that I might be sitting at home feeling sorry for myself the following morning in familiar surroundings.

The Head of the clinic paid her early morning visit and frightened the crap out of me as usual. The first nurse of the day to arrive at my bedside put a slightly less stressful look on my face. She was accompanied by the same physiotherapist who had examined me on my arrival. It became apparent that her initial impression was that the problems caused by the injuries to my back and the jolt to my brain were not going to improve rapidly by leaving me lying on a hospital bed staring at the ceiling. She went on to explain that after that first examination she had stressed that fact to the powers that be and recommended that I be allowed to return home, where I could move around freely and think things over rather than worrying about which part of my body the next needle would be invading! That line of thinking was what I myself had been desperately trying to put over since my return to sanity back in Leipzig.

After the physiotherapist had finished her by then familiar tapping of my joints with a small mallet, she furrowed her brow and made her way to the next patient after telling me to arrange for somebody to come and collect me later that day. Although I hadn't been there long she was concerned about my lack of mobility. I would recover quicker where I would have to fetch and carry for myself.

My call home wasn't a long one. Unfortunately there was nobody in, and so the answer machine listened to twenty seconds of excited waffle. I tried to say that I would call back later and tell my father exactly what time to collect me.

The seconds turned to hours and the hours turned to decades. By the middle of the afternoon there was still no word and then the physiotherapist reappeared still wearing that furrowed brow. The happiness that had been about to explode inside me jogged off down a side-street and watched from a distance. 'I hope you haven't arranged anything yet,' she said. 'You could be here another few days.'

My happiness evaporated, to be replaced by anger heading straight for my fists, only to be overtaken by despair. I sank back on to the bed and just waited and waited. Waiting was something that had become second nature to me. Despite being just a shade upset by having my hopes built up to such a high level and swiftly demolished, sitting on a bed in my home town didn't seem anywhere near as bad as enduring the same pursuit in Leipzig – almost enjoyable in fact in a funny 'stuffing my face full of chocolate' kind of way!

Another phone call was duly made, leaving a message to ignore the information I had barked at the answer phone not fifteen minutes previously. My mind was immediately turned away from the bad news by the arrival of my brother. After ten minutes of joking, I had cheered up to such an extent that I had completely forgotten what I had been so down about in the first place. It wasn't long before the reminder came when my father telephoned, asking me to explain fully what I had garbled down the phone. After describing the events of the previous ninety minutes, any further discussion was saved until his visit that evening.

Later that day my mother's daily visit was in full swing when I was informed that the nice neuropsychologist was ready to see me to assess my mental state and then give the final okay to my return home if he saw fit. I still had the rehearsed script that I had spent the night learning fresh in my mind. I went over it once more as I made the short trip to his office.

Sitting in the comfortable chair in front of him, I couldn't help but notice that he was staring at me intently. That was set to continue throughout our discussion. Even though that unnerving behaviour was simply to assess my body language, I became even more nervous than I had been on entering his office. His first acknowledgement of my presence was to point out that I must be either worried or tense as I apparently had my hands clenched tightly together. Nerves set in.

My first impression was that I could probably just sit in silence for as long as it took him to work out all of my thoughts by simply watching me twitch nervously in my chair. My theory proved false as the questioning began.

'What happened?'

'Can you remember anything?'

'How do you feel?'

'Do you feel any bitterness towards the events or the people involved?'

His actual words were ones which I fortunately grasped the meaning of without the aid of a dictionary – a feat in itself and probably a cunning part of his assessment. I then started to answer all the aforementioned questions. My script seemed to be working successfully as he failed to dwell on any of my answers. Surely that was a sign that I was saying what he wanted to hear?

He had obviously been happy with what he had heard when he shook one of my hands and placed a list of appointments in the other. 'We have decided to let you go home tonight,' he said.

Whoop!

Home is something which for most of the time is taken for granted. It had become much more that evening and I wouldn't be exaggerating by saying the psychologist's announcement was without doubt the happiest moment of my life. Knowing that my next destination was my own bed seemed to signal the end of the ordeal and a return to normality at last. The worst was over and, after all, it had been such a long time since I had received one of those slaps in the face, so frequent in Germany. It was going to be easy from here on in. The truth was that the easy part had just finished and the real work would be getting under way very soon and it would not be for me alone.

Not surprisingly, I never thought I would feel excited at the prospect of walking into my own kitchen. That evening, though, it was. After ten minutes of sitting on a comfortable chair with a steaming hot mug of coffee at my side, I at last understood the meaning of the word 'familiar'.

It is only when the day-to-day life that you are accustomed to disappears, that you suddenly start to appreciate what was there in the first place. You then find yourself driving down a one-way street. You smile and wave to everything and everyone you know, while all the while approaching your own personal brick wall at the very end of the street. It wasn't very long before I crashed head first into my own. I realised all to soon that I had come so very close to not seeing any of my street again. I didn't smile to myself and mentally shake my own hand. I sat very, very still, thought for a moment and frightened myself stupid. Through all that had occurred in the previous weeks, I had at no point been at all brave or indeed had the tiniest amount of determination to pull through and recover. I hadn't had a clue what had been going on most of the time and even after my return to consciousness my mind had not been my own for most of it, so therefore I had simply been extremely lucky.

On that first night home I couldn't help but think about that fifty-fifty chance. For some unexplained reason I couldn't think about my good fortune and instead spent weeks just feeling incredibly humble and very small indeed. I just could not explain why I had been one of the lucky ones who fate decides should have another chance.

My personal brick wall was to take some time to pull down and break up. You do eventually get there, but there is always the pile of rubble in the background to remind you what was there and no amount of removal will ever clear it away totally. I soon decided that instead of staring at the remains and letting it drag me down, I would occasionally give it a quick glance and laugh at it instead. It was easier for anyone who knew me to approach the topic with a tasteless joke rather than talking to me as if I was some kind of hero, when all I had done was wake up one morning and be told what had happened and that the worst was over – hardly heroic. It wasn't very long before the subject didn't affect me at all and I could quite happily talk about it to anyone who wanted to hear but I was not really in the mood to sit around dwelling on the past. I was now back at home and able to circulate, albeit in a limited capacity. The plan was to spend as much time as I could away from anywhere medical and to once again appreciate everyone around me.

The first two days back home were spent visiting friends and family with Lucy on my arm. Lucy was ready to talk to me whenever I felt a little down. Talking was to take up much of my time as I had no desire to be spending hours sat in pubs or to be boogying the night away in nightclubs. Social calls had been limited to minutes rather than hours due to the intense tiredness that washed over me during periods of activity. If just talking was enough to make me pine for my comfortable mattress, then drinking and dancing were not top of my priority list. I would often be forced midway through the day to retire into my shell for an hour and once again recharge my batteries. These daylight periods of sleep would prepare me for the main course every night, which consisted of at least ten hours of blissful unawareness. This was not by choice, it was a necessity if I wanted to wake up feeling anything other than unwell.

During one particularly sumptuous main course of sleep came the most bizarre experience, not only of my rehabilitation, but also of my whole life. I dreamed a saga that was so clear, I knew instantly on waking up that it had been far too familiar for me to have experienced it for the first time.

I had, without a doubt, had the very same dream in the past, yet could not recall when. Then after a great deal of thought I realised. That dream had been no normal dream. It was too clear and I could also remember parts of the dream that hadn't occurred in my sleep the previous night. My almost lifeless, comatose brain, despite its period of inactivity had still been able to spring upon me what I am convinced had been a 'near-death experience'. I had no awareness of a light at the end of a tunnel and there were no deceased friends to call me through it. My story, far from falling into the cliché, was more comical. I had entered a large dining area to find the biggest table I had ever seen. Sitting upon each chair surrounding the table was a relative or friend. Every chair was taken and everyone I cared about was there – a lifetime of acquaintances all gathered at one spot at the same time, with the largest meal I had ever seen in front of each one of them. I was ushered to my seat at the head of the table by a stranger and told to wait. I sat down and noticed immediately that the only person without any food was myself. After a long wait involving much conversation with my fellow diners, the usher returned to inform me that I had to fetch my meal and return to the gathering before a countdown expired. A twist in the tale was that if I failed to return before the clock reached zero, I would die. No second chance; quite simply, death awaited.

Next came panic, sheer unadulterated panic. I was rushing from room to room in a state of terror and it did not feel like dreaming. It was real to me, very real. I eventually found my meal and made it back before the countdown expired. I eventually awoke to find that the nearest I had come to death was drowning in my own sweat, at least on that second occasion! I climbed out of bed and spent a lot of time trying to make sense of what had just occurred. I began to shake as I considered the outcome of the dream back in Germany, and what if the second hand of the clock had reached zero before I had managed to return to my friends around that table. It is probably as well that I will always remain ignorant of the answer. Is the human brain complex enough to know when it is going to die and send the rest of your body a message in story form to warn it? I was slightly worried by my brain's choice of story of death or food! Not exactly Oscar-winning stuff, yet it was immensely frightening to me. For a short while I even lost my appetite!

Having experienced a reminder of what I had come so close to, I became aware of the urgent need to let go of any hurt or anguish surrounding the events of December '94. It was at that point that I chose the wrong route to recovery. I simply decided there and then that I would forget all about it and that the aforementioned hurt and anguish could take a back seat and watch as I recovered. I would return to everything in my life that I had enjoyed so much prior to the accident. However much I tried to persuade myself that I didn't have a care in the world that time wouldn't heal, I was merely shutting the truth out. Silence isn't golden, after all. It is in fact tarnished to such an extent, that the longer I chose to ignore it, the more difficult it would be to clean away.

It was obvious, on reflection, that it was only a matter of time before my emotions could no longer take the strain and I would erupt. That could perhaps be avoided if my life was to run smoothly in the first months after my discharge. That would surely be the case, wouldn't it? Everyone I knew was overjoyed to have me back home, any therapy I would need would not be a strain and I had a girlfriend who had agreed to be my wife. The hand that had done all that slapping must have had enough. Nothing could go wrong – could it? Not really very likely, was it?

The following two months became a routine of hospital visits and house calls to friends until one fateful day when my pangs for alcohol awoke with a vengeance as I returned from a routine therapy session. My father, never being one to shy from the odd drink, pulled up at the local watering hole and in we went. I like to think that I am a sensible and responsible individual when it comes to my own health. I knew that alcohol was not going to help my brain. It does not take a high IQ to understand that a substance which sets about slaughtering your perception, co-ordination and plain rational thinking was not going to help me in any way, shape or form. But maybe I was wrong about being responsible and sensible.

As I finished my tenth cigarette of the day, I drank a mouthful from my second bottle of beer and continued to chat with my father about Lucy and our plans for the future. Since my return she had been a rock. She had made sure that she was there every day for company which was a huge help alone. For a month she stayed away from her friends simply to spend time with me. I tried to tell her to spend time away whilst all the time knowing that I didn't really want her to and also knowing that she was aware of that. She would arrive every day to the same scenario. I would be happy to see her yet unable to do the things that were second nature due to severe tiredness and a combination of problems resulting from my brain injury. She had been aware of that and happily gone along with my wishes. She had understood everything and been very special to me.

The only question to answer now was whether or not Lucy, or indeed any of the people around me, did really understand. Were they simply saying they did to reassure me in the same way as I was pretending not to feel any anger towards the events leading to my predicament? Lucy was seeing me, accompanying me to the hospital when I needed to go and she assumed that that was enough to understand completely what was happening to me. That must be very easy to do but merely being with the person can never be enough. On one side of the coin I hid my thoughts from her and on the other, she from me. The coin was heading towards the ground at a tremendous speed and when it finally hit, the chances of us remaining in the same way of thinking and loving that we had at that time or alternatively falling apart were as even as the flip of a coin.

As the days passed by, I began to notice subtle changes in Lucy's behaviour, the kind of changes that could only be spotted by someone who knew her extremely well.

It had still been only three months since my return when the first sign of trouble reared up and kicked me in the teeth. Lucy had a free day and by pure coincidence, I had no appointment at the hospital. My highly qualified therapist had seen fit to give me a short break from making the trip. (After all, at that time all my therapy involved was playing Connect Four with my left hand in a bid to correct, or at least help, my co-ordination problems. In retrospect, it makes sense but it seemed so childish and annoying at the time.) My relief at avoiding that little delight for once led me to confront my lack of confidence and suggest to Lucy a visit to the nearest seaside resort, a forty-mile drive away. Maybe the sea air would do me some good and just getting away, if only for a day, was a pleasant thought. Lucy agreed and into the car we jumped, just me, Lucy and a pack of cigarettes.

The hour's drive was totally uneventful. A 'T-shirt' mentality filled the car. The windows were down, the radio was loud and laughter filled the air. The sun was shining and it really was a very nice day – an almost unique event. The traffic became steadily busier and busier the nearer we got to our destination. By the time we arrived, it was teeming with people. It seemed that everybody within a forty-mile radius of the place had had the very same idea and had all arrived together. As we headed off to find the nearest parking space, I looked around, took in the sight of what looked to me like the population of the country on one street and Mr Brain screamed out, 'No!' No warning and no immediate reasoning – just a blunt no! I simply could not take it all in and started to panic. Lucy looked across at me sitting, staring blankly and said – nothing. I quickly informed her of the unlikelihood of me getting out of the car and asked her to turn the car around and head for home. As soon as we were clear of the town, I felt a huge surge of relief.

Since my return to England I had spent the time getting out as much as possible while all the time hiding a rather large slice of anxiety as far back in my mind as I could. On that particular day, my anxiety had decided to put up a bit of a fight and on arriving at the town the towel had been thrown in. Rather than spending three months being a tiny bit anxious all the time, I had hidden it away completely and it had all formed into one huge problem which eventually became too large for me to cope with any more. When the fuse was lit, there was always going to be one big bang.

It was an experience that I had never staggered across before, which was precisely why it was a turning point for me. Carrying around a little anxiety at all times is not an obstacle if it is kept at a realistic level. Too much anxiety and your life becomes far too fearful to contemplate carrying on in the same way. The longer you carry on in that way, the more difficult it is to turn the corner. I had turned the corner almost overnight. I had been hiding behind the smile of a man who was only too pleased to be alive to let my anxiety affect me. Then, in the blink of an eye, the whole recipe for disaster reached boiling point and raised a couple of fingers in my direction.

It was the most difficult hour that I spent in those first weeks. Immediately afterwards all I wanted to do was go home and stay there with the doors locked. For those few minutes in Lucy's car I had no feelings for anyone other than myself and I wanted it to stay that way. I sat rigid and totally silent and felt all the anxiety drift away. I felt so much calmer and set about attempting to explain the whole sorry episode to a perplexed Lucy who was sitting in the same rigid and silent manner. I was soon to discover that our similar postures were for far from similar reasons. The rest of that day was spent with one of us discussing the relief that had come from a completely wasted day and the other expressing what I can only describe as disgust at having to drive for an hour, sit in silence for fifteen minutes and then promptly turn the car around and head back to square one. Three hours had been wasted achieving nothing at all.

In actual fact it had been a very productive three hours for me. As for square one, as I had moved a distance in front of it, our partnership had ended up miles behind it, possibly too far away for us to reach again.

I hoped more than anything that in time Lucy would see that I was no longer able to participate in activities that before I had taken for granted. For me it was extremely difficult to feel like I was the same person, both physically and mentally, who had stepped on to that ferry months previously with every intention of working for the money that would enable me to start a new life with Lucy. I *was* the same person but realised very quickly that I would have to adjust. I was trying very hard because I had to, yet it seemed to me that Lucy was not really paying any attention. Fifteen minutes sat in a car at the seafront had taught me more about her attitude towards my predicament than any of the time we had spent together since my arrival home. It became apparent that she had fallen into the trap of thinking that I was slowly returning to my former self, and that she was paying no attention to anything other than the highs. When the lows inevitably appeared, it wasn't much fun any more. The euphoria of my survival had been slowly replaced by the harsh truth. She was realising that the near future would not be all smiles after all. It was not going to be easy for her, now that an example of the real me that had been hidden under the bravado had decided to reveal itself, and a clearer picture was beginning to develop. Show a picture to a hundred different people and some will like it. Others, however, will not see anything worth looking at. After that episode it seemed as though Lucy was squinting in a desperate bid to find the part of the picture that pleased her and she was struggling.

It is not selfish for any of us to want nothing other than good for ourselves at all times. Nobody chooses to have a life that's riddled with struggle. You are indeed a lucky person if you succeed in avoiding the bad times for the whole of your life. I have no idea how my outlook on life would have been affected had it been Lucy who had fallen down that stairwell instead of me and I never will. I can't even try to imagine how you must feel when you are faced with someone else's trauma every day and have no idea whether the future will get any better. Initially, all is well but if there is no improvement as time passes, it can all become too much and some may simply walk away. Lucy was beginning to look as if she would be joining that category and a warning bell was ringing in the distance. The immediate future was destined to be a trying time for both of us.

More quiet, uneventful days passed by, in fact, just the sort of days that I desperately needed as I had been warned by various specialists not to up the tempo too soon. There was no point in going to extremes so soon after my return. Like many ailments, plenty of rest and sleep plays an important part. There is just one tiny flaw – it can eventually become incredibly boring and so Lucy's continued patience despite the previous events was much appreciated. Everyone had been brilliant back at home; the family, my friends and even Christian and Romy back in Leipzig were still telephoning almost every week. It was all very nice, and the attention was always welcome yet it was Lucy who was the important piece of the jigsaw. I had stood back and put our altercation to the back of my mind, hoping that it may have been a one off and the one that made her think. Nothing was going to go wrong. I had lived through the worst and it was all up from here on. It hadn't even entered my mind that Lucy would not be there if I needed her.

What I hadn't stopped to think about was that three or four hours of company and occasionally driving me to hospital was easy for her. There would eventually come a time when the thought of spending twenty-four hours a day with someone who was relying on her to be there would enter her mind. You have to confront your feelings towards that person and any doubts that may then appear. After that, it is very easy to hide behind the excuse that you just can't handle the consequences of the accident or whatever, and it seemed so obvious that that was happening with Lucy.

During one particular appointment at the hospital with the neuropsychologist, he decided to ask Lucy to come along with me on my next visit. He would talk to her about how the accident had affected her and her outlook on the future with me. It seemed strange to me that this suggestion was made after I had been at home for three months. Surely it would have been better to have done this earlier so she could have been given an idea what to expect from me. No matter, at last he had decided to talk to Lucy and maybe she would feel better about the situation after discussing her thoughts with him.

I was happy that at long last my loved ones were being addressed. After all, they had been equally traumatised. While I had stumbled on through, simply following instructions because I was either unconscious, unaware or simply had no choice, it had been the people around me who had been faced with the worry and anguish. These are states of mind that are never pleasant for a few seconds even; obviously a few months is far more difficult to handle. An experienced counsellor advising all concerned may well have helped or it might not have, but it was worth a try.

My next visit to the hospital would enable the specialists to examine the extent of my recovery up to that point. I was to face the same set of tests that I had done on my arrival from Germany. Comparing the results would give them, and more importantly me, a clear view of which parts of my brain had enjoyed their little holiday and decided that the time was ripe to get back to work. For obvious reasons, I was a shade nervous about learning the outcome. I was convinced I was doing well, to the extent that myself and Lucy had made arrangements to celebrate my recovery by going out that night. I had warned Lucy in advance that there was a chance I may not feel like enjoying the evening if it was to be bad news I learnt from the hospital.

The morning of the tests arrived and I made my way to hospital in a cautious mood. I had successfully overcome my anxiety and possessed a new-found confidence which I hoped to use to good effect whilst performing the mental tasks set before me as tests. I sat down and the thirty minutes it took to complete the tasks passed quickly. A smile began to appear on my face. Just as the smile was about to turn into a full-blown smug grin, the hand that had become so familiar to me, reared up and gave me another solid slap.

I was informed of the results. During the first three months of my rehabilitation I had improved not one jot. The tests had been completed almost identically to how I had performed on that very first day. I suddenly realised that I was probably wasting my time in my efforts to return to 'normal'. I was determined that I would not feel sorry for myself, I would still go out with Lucy that night, but I would have to try to explain why I was so down. Cue warning number two.

By coincidence, that night we would also be celebrating the birthday of one of Lucy's friends. After explaining to her the outcome of my tests I was told that that night was not the night to talk about it and could I please just stay quiet and enjoy myself. Ho, ho, ho.

Needless to say, it wasn't the most enjoyable night of my life. I sat observing everyone having a whale of a time and leaving me to dwell on the events of eight hours previously. I couldn't possibly concentrate on having fun despite having every intention to do just that only the day before. There was too much whirling around in my head that seemed too important to think about anything else. The, determination I had to forget what had occurred had waned the moment I stepped out of the door. Lucy only saw this as selfish. I was spending far too much time thinking about myself. That was undoubtedly true, but I had to. How could I ever start to get back to normal unless I spent the majority of my time concentrating on it? Along with the ups would also come the downs and I had to successfully pull through those as well. Lucy was always there with a reward when the ups came along. As soon as a down showed itself, it all became a bit boring to her. Who wants to sit around being miserable when you can go somewhere else and have a good time?

I was still convinced that Lucy would soon see that I could not help my behaviour and that things would improve. I needed them to. The following day that slapping hand took a day off and reached for a hammer. Since I had returned home, between Lucy and myself had been a coffin with a large nail hovering above it. The hammer was hurtling down towards the nail and threatening to strike it very hard indeed. There were already countless nails in the coffin that was our relationship, but that was indeed the final one.

Lucy arrived at my home that afternoon to pick me up and go out to do something as trivial as shopping! I had known we were going, yet when the time arrived, I had lost my confidence and told her I could not go. All of my co-ordination had deserted me, I had a throbbing headache and was in no state to wander around crowded shops. No comforting arm appeared round my shoulder and I certainly hadn't prepared myself for what followed.

'Pull yourself together!', 'Speed yourself up!', 'Get a grip!', were just three of the things shouted at me in what to me was an almost vicious manner. All of my hurt, along with a tiny bit of shame poured out in the form of tears for the next hour; a twenty-five year old man having a complete emotional breakdown compressed into one hour. Lucy either could not, or would not, understand and soon decided that two weeks apart may help. I could not see how avoiding me would help, but still agreed to it in the hope that it might just work.

A single week passed by and my reacquaintance with alcohol took priority. Numerous people joined me as I was drowning in huge amounts of personal misery. For a short while all of my consolation came in a glass and the more I drank, the better I felt. I felt better, because I would forget what I was so miserable about in the first place. It didn't last though. Ten days into our agreed temporary break, I found myself missing Lucy and picked the phone up for a chat. A distant voice greeted me at the other end of the line. I cheerfully enquired about how she was and what she was doing. Then out of the blue and without warning, I heard, 'Listen, this is not working. I think it's best if we don't see each other any more.'

No affection, no apology, and no explanation. An agreement was made to meet the following day in order to exchange personal belongings and that would be it. The meeting took place and still with no explanation for the split we parted amicably – at least from her side.

Four days after the split, a mutual friend observed Lucy in the middle of town in what can only be described as intimate conversation with a man who turned into her housemate three days later. Six months and twenty-three days after the accident, four months of almost constant support and two months of being engaged and it suddenly died. Her distress was so completely overwhelming that she had felt the need to find a new man.

Right up there at the forefront of my mind now sat shock, sadness, hurt, bitterness, disgust and more than a little hatred. I was lower than I had ever been. The one person I so desperately needed had walked away. As the hours passed, the more the hatred built up inside. However, all the time I knew I would never really hate her, but I would always hate and never forget what she had done.

Within two days, everything I possessed that could remind me of Lucy in any way had been destroyed. Photographs, letters, etc., all gone; not a trace remained. From love to hate in one sentence, that's all it took. That hammer had struck the final nail into the coffin, yet it would take weeks to drive it home. Only one week had passed when her first contact was made, a brief telephone call, still with no explanations, just a reminder of a small amount of money I had borrowed about three years previously. Perhaps after that she would leave me alone. No, those slaps would keep on coming for some time.

After all my experiences with hiding away my anxiety and hurt instead of coming to terms with it, I still hadn't learned and it started all over again. The two weeks after our split were spent convincing myself that I had always hated Lucy, that we never had any good times and that I wasn't hurting at all. You can only kid yourself for so long though before you realise the truth and confront it.

There was only one month of depression to kill before one of the biggest slaps I received took my mind off the past completely. However, I did still have to kill that month and so once more, the local bars became my second home. I was finding it strange that when I was upset at home not many of my acquaintances wanted to know, yet when I chose to dwell on my sorrows over a few drinks, suddenly people became concerned. It is so much easier for someone to listen to your troubles when you can share a drink or two. It is the other waking hours that are the difficult ones and the time when you really need the company.

For me there were a few stalwarts who were prepared to sacrifice their time to try and cheer me up and help me through. My brother who had been trying to do just that when I was comatose, must have been sick of the sight of me, as he was almost always there. For him those weeks must have seemed easy after his visits to the hospital when he had been trying for days without success to get me simply to acknowledge his presence. Favours were also owed to a father who often dragged me out of my permanent position sat miserably on my bed and a mother who was forever prepared to listen to my inane ramblings until the early hours of the morning almost every night of the week.

When you are desperately in need of something to look forward to, it isn't often that something occurs that enables you to forget the previous few days and concentrate on that instead. At long last, Lady Luck decided to pay me a visit.

The telephone rang and just as I was bracing myself to hurl a stream of obscenities down the line to Lucy, a familiar voice with a distinctly Teutonic accent greeted me cheerfully. It was Christian! He asked about my state of health and of any improvement, and ended the conversation with an announcement. He would be visiting England ten days later. A rare smile appeared on my face. The last time I had seen Christian I hadn't been very good company for him. Nevertheless, he had helped me and my family during the worst days and I couldn't wait to spend a weekend with him on my own turf and catch up on the goings on back in the nightclub. In an instant, my thoughts turned from being down about my relationship breaking up, to being excited at the prospect of seeing my old mate again. However, I was slightly perturbed after he had informed me that he would be bringing three friends with him who I had never met. Never mind – any friend of Christian had to be a friend of mine.

The news spread quickly and we realised that even though Christian's flat in Leipzig had been home to several of my friends and relatives during my days in hospital, only my parents and my brother had actually met him. Lucy had spent a few nights talking to him, but for obvious reasons any friendship they may have had would not be rekindled on his visit to our country. Everybody was looking forward to seeing him. Back in Leipzig, he had softened the blow for everyone with his undying ability to be extremely friendly and cheerful at all times. Now we could repay a bit of that friendship on his visit.

By pure coincidence, George would be flying home the very same day as Christian would be arriving. He would also visit to add yet more enjoyment to the weekend. George and myself had become good mates during our trips to Christian's nightclub and during the hours that we were supposed to be working, and some of the time when we actually were. He had kept in touch with me in the months since the accident with at least one phone call every week and so it would also be good to see him again.

Chapter Nine

One in Twenty

The week preceding the combined visits passed by quietly. The usual dull days were not even being punctuated by sessions of therapy at the hospital any more. As far as my problems with co-ordination were concerned, the specialists had decided that they had done all they could for the time being. The neuropsychologist had left me with the understanding that we would only talk if I felt the need to discuss any problems, thereby avoiding pointless journeys to the hospital.

The only problem remaining, that had so far been unchecked, was my eyesight. Along with the other problems that the left side of my body had, I had also lost part of my left-hand field of vision. Although I was aware of this, as yet I had not had a proper ophthalmic examination. People could creep up on me from the left and I would not see them until they were two inches away. On one occasion, I had bent over to pick something up off the floor and hadn't seen a waist-high cupboard six inches to my left and almost knocked myself unconscious as a still fragile head connected with it. Even more worrying, was that there was no explanation for the events of two days later. I was standing in the garden with a friend when my father ventured towards me from the left. He then disappeared and instantly reappeared, coming towards me again in exactly the same fashion and that happened five or six times. I explained what was happening to a more than perplexed friend who said that my father was at that time not even in the garden, and was in fact inside the house.

Waves of nausea swept over me, soon followed by a throbbing migraine. A doctor was called for, who could find no explanation for the hallucinations that seemed to trigger the sickness. I am no medical expert yet I have my own theory. The previous day I had been for an appointment at an eye clinic as I was more than a little worried about my vision, far more worried than the specialists at the hospital seemed to be. After mentioning my worries for the sixth time, an appointment had at last been made to assess the extent of the problem. I had undergone a field of vision test which involved looking at flashing and flickering lights which would be uncomfortable at the best of times. It wasn't an enjoyable ten minutes and I had no desire to sit through it again. Twenty-four hours after that dubious pleasure came the garden hallucinations. Coincidence? No one was prepared to say one way or the other, but the hallucinations were certainly a warning for what was to come. That little episode had almost been forgotten by the time of the German invasion of our home. It was to become significant by the time the visit had ended.

The evening of the much anticipated arrival came and I prepared myself for the fun that was to come, despite the fact that George had already telephoned to tell me that, true to form, he had missed his flight. Typical George. Still, there would be plenty of catching up to do with Christian. A car arrived outside the house late that evening and an extremely happy Christian clambered out to be greeted by hugs from myself and my parents who were undoubtedly just as pleased to see him as I was. We were hurriedly introduced to the three girls he had brought over with him, two cousins and a friend. The females were duly despatched to their beds while Christian and myself sat until the early hours of the morning.

Eventually we got some sleep and the morning arrived. I stumbled through to the kitchen feeling a little the worse for wear. On top of the tiredness, I also felt just a tiny bit ill. I missed breakfast and didn't feel like being particularly friendly to our guests. Unfortunately, I simply couldn't socialise in any way and wandered outside with my father for some fresh air.

Suddenly my vision failed me totally. I could see everything clearly but it was all appearing in the wrong place; everything on the left appeared to the right and vice versa. I was struck by confusion and a touch of panic. My father sensed a problem and sat me down safely indoors. My panic progressed through into outright fear when I then completely lost control of both legs. That sensation proceeded to spread throughout my entire body until it could take no more. I could feel my heart pounding like a bass drum and then – nothing. In my mind I had gone in the blink of an eye from shaking uncontrollably on a chair, to being flat out in the back of an ambulance with my mother and an ambulance man talking in muffled voices about 'epileptic seizures'. I had approached those three doors when comatose and exited through the one marked 'lucky bastard'. Now I was confronted by the subtext at the bottom of the sign, that I hadn't paid any attention to. 'One in twenty people who suffer head injuries develop epilepsy.' One in twenty; I had to be one of them. I had plenty of time to ponder it, but all I cared about at that time was the headache I had that felt like nothing short of a brain tumour. The expected weekend of fun had died.

The last time Christian had seen me in Leipzig I had been in a hospital. Then he travelled almost a thousand miles, had spoken to me for a couple of hours or so and I was – in a hospital again. It might have felt like home to him. Christian, along with my still ever-present brother spent the rest of that day next to my bed in hospital trying to perk me up again, a situation that the two of them had hoped they would never have to sit through again. As they attempted to cheer me it became clear that it wasn't as difficult to achieve as they imagined. Everyone who suffers from epilepsy has different experiences during and after a seizure. On that occasion, recovering from my first seizure was similar to waking from my coma – some illness and a tremendous amount of confusion. I had blacked out during the seizure and had no recollection of what had happened to me after I had begun to shake uncontrollably back at home.

The doctors at the hospital decided to keep me under observation that night and allowed me to return home the next morning. I was told not to worry and to get on with my life to the best of my ability. The head injury that I had suffered wasn't necessarily the reason for the seizure. Anybody, young, old, sick or healthy can at any time suffer a seizure, so there really wasn't that much for the doctors to worry about. If there ever came a time when a second seizure showed up at the party, then that would be the time to gather around and talk 'medication'.

I arrived home that morning to be greeted by our German visitors. I still wasn't fully aware of what had happened the day before and had no desire to spend my time worrying about it happening again as Christian with his group would be travelling home the next day. We did manage to spend the final night of their visit at the local bar reminiscing and having a good time. All too soon though, the night ended, the alarm clock rang in the morning and they were all on their way, leaving me to sit alone and think rationally about the weekend.

I thought all I could and failed to make any sense of it at all. Why had I been okay for nine months? What had caused the seizure? Would it happen again, and could I prevent it? What I had thought was going to be a fun weekend had, in fact, left me with a whole new set of problems to get my head around. I now quite possibly had epilepsy which could strike at any time without warning, just as it had during Christian's visit. However, I wasn't dying. People have far more serious ailments to contend with and it might not even happen again.

Amazingly, I managed to hide it away at the back of my mind. I chose to believe that it had been mere coincidence and would never happen again and within a week I was back to my usual self. That was definitely where my fortunes would start to change. There was no chance of me suffering another seizure as I had used up all my share of bad luck and now the tide had turned. What was that about being slapped?

Life returned to the same routine of sleeping, eating, drinking and sleeping again with the occasional excursion to the local golf club for some exercise. Eventually, the pattern was broken when a month later a friend called and asked if I would like to take a trip out with him as his work involved a lot of travelling. I agreed and jumped into the car, more for a change than for pleasure.

The day was drawing to a close when out of the corner of my eye I saw my mate on the opposite side of the car to where he was sitting. This time I recognised the signs instantly and kept talking to take my mind off what was happening. By the time we stopped so I could have a breath of fresh air I had staved it off entirely. I opened my tightly shut eyes and saw once again – my mother with the very same ambulance man finishing off their conversation about epileptic seizures. I had not staved it off as I had believed and in actual fact, I had blacked out and suffered another full-blown seizure.

The theory that anybody could suffer one seizure no longer applied in my case. I was now officially suffering from epilepsy. Those hallucinations that had taken place in the garden weeks previously now had an explanation. I had in fact been extremely lucky on that occasion as my brain had chosen not to take the hallucinations one step further into a seizure. They were merely a warning, that strangely no one could see. Each case involving epilepsy is very different to the next. A warning of a seizure will usually show itself to whoever is about to have it. This is known as an 'aura' and can be very similar to each other yet two people rarely have the same one. It becomes a learning process. Knowing when the strange experience you are having is going to develop into a seizure is quite difficult when it is all very new to you. At least I was then aware that if I was to start hallucinating badly, it most probably meant that I was about to succumb again. Other unusual occurrences that I had spent the best part of my recovery trying to ignore now had a reason.

Ever since my return home there had been occasions when I would fall into a trance-like state for a second or two, then as quickly as it had started I would be fully aware once more. In a way it was pleasing to know why and that I wasn't going mad as I had occasionally feared. Although I was aware of what the problem was now, it had all come to a head in a very short space of time. Almost overnight my rehabilitation had been hampered by the fresh knowledge that at any time at all there was a possibility that I could awake, open my eyes and not have the faintest idea of where I was or how I had got there.

Fortunately for me, after those first seizures either a friend or a member of the family had been with me to explain what had happened as soon as I regained consciousness. I would come out of the seizure and be in a state of confusion. All I understood was just how violent the headache I was suffering was. Having somebody at close quarters to talk to me after the event was a life saver in those early days, when I wasn't sure myself what had happened.

After the second seizure I had been, once again, rushed to the local hospital. Rather than keeping me in overnight for observation as they had done previously, that time I was treated almost nonchalantly. I was told to contact my doctor at the first available opportunity and was allowed to return home within the hour. The final instruction given to me was that if I ever suffered a further seizure there was no reason to call an ambulance, but just to let things take their natural course. A visit to my doctor would enable him to prescribe medication that could, with a slice of luck, prevent anything untoward happening to me in the future.

This piece of good news was what I really wanted to hear. Removing the threat that I would suffer further seizures would have taken away a bit of the worry and given me yet more confidence to carry on with my attempt to return to my former life. But it's not quite that easy. There are numerous drugs available on prescription for epilepsy and any one of them may control it. There is also an equal chance that not one single one will work. Easy! I would just work my way through all of them until I found one that successfully prevented me from having any further seizures. It was at this point in the proceedings that I began to wish that I had tried a lot harder at school and gone on to be a doctor instead of a 'glamour' job in the building trade.

On top of having a great deal of choice when it came to medication, there was the problem that a drug may well work at a very low dosage, but again it may not. If, despite the medication, another seizure happens the dosage is raised and so on until it can go no higher and a completely new drug must be tried.

I thought it would be an easy task. It could never be an easy or indeed speedy procedure though, as my seizures tended to be weeks apart and so the attempts to find the right drug would be a long haul. To make the situation even more frustrating, you can never be one hundred per cent sure that you will not suffer another seizure, even it's been years since the last one. As I have said before, the brain is an extremely complex piece of equipment and, after all, there was always the chance that I could suffer a seizure for the same reasons as anyone could.

Some people may find the control required with the first medication prescribed to them and some may never get their epilepsy under control. It is a condition which can be very uncomfortable when it strikes, but once again it cannot be stressed enough that only rarely is it a dangerous condition. It shouldn't alter your life in circumstances such as my own. As I only suffered seizures every few weeks and not, as in some cases, two or three times a day, that is easy for me to say. I can't even begin to understand just how uncomfortable epilepsy must be when you have problems on a daily basis, and even sometimes on an hourly basis.

Almost before I had begun to understand the condition, the stigma attached to it started to enter my mind. When the word 'epilepsy' was first mentioned, I immediately remembered a child at school who suffered with it. We had all been extremely cruel and dubbed him as weird and called him many, many very hurtful names. On reaching adulthood I had always felt tremendously guilty at how we had made his life that much harder, yet when I began to suffer seizures myself, strangely the guilt disappeared. It soon became abundantly clear that the vast majority of the people surrounding me had very little knowledge of what to expect and how to react. If adults struggled, then how on earth can children be expected to see someone who has epilepsy as anything other than a freak?

After all, it is easy to be around someone who simply has headaches and feels unwell spasmodically. It's a whole new ball game when you have to contend with a person who behaves exactly how you expect them to, talking, sharing a joke, simply being themselves and one minute later having very little understanding of who you are or what you are saying and doing. Finally, there is also the possibility that the person concerned may completely lose control of his body for a few seconds, seize up totally and fall unconscious for a while. To the uneducated, this can seem to be very antisocial behaviour, particularly when they learn that there is no way of knowing where and when it will strike. You can be cocooned in the privacy of your own home, sat in the bar, watching a football match, in fact anywhere at all. All your friends or an observer can do to help is let the seizure run its course. Waiting is the only course of action. It is that easy. An ambulance is not required and the condition certainly isn't contagious, so why the stigma? Maybe embarrassment. There is something about having no control over a problem that frightens us a little. That of course, and the threat of a friend doing a session of 'horizontal break-dancing' can make people wary. This is despite the fact that, apart from these ten minute interludes, you are no different from the person you were before epilepsy came to play a part in your life.

Lucy had decided to get away two months previously and for her it had turned out to be a good move. If it was true, as most of us suspected, that she found it too difficult and stressful to cope after my homecoming, then she had timed her escape to perfection. After my discharge from hospital I had been confused, lethargic, my co-ordination had been shot to pieces and I suffered the odd migraine. It sounds strange, but other than those problems I was fine. I would visit my specialists twice a week for sessions of therapy, return home and spend as much time as possible with Lucy. If that had been too much for her to contend with, then a nervous breakdown would have been the next logical step for her on discovering I had epilepsy. I can't imagine the reaction had I actually had a seizure whilst I was with her and I will never know. If there could ever have been a good time to learn of my epilepsy, it had come at just the right moment. My relationship breaking up came a distant second place compared to worrying about my new health concerns. Anyway, I had far more serious things to spend my time thinking about than what Lucy might have been up to. I had had two seizures and was in the middle of trying to be normal, while the doctors were trying even harder to find a suitable medication quickly. I was starting all over again. I had tried it once and the epilepsy had forced me back into that square marked with a bold 'one'.

My confidence had deserted me yet again and I had to build it up once more. That meant taking everything slowly and only doing things when I felt ready to do them; there was no point rushing.

Lucy had gone and the stigma attached to epilepsy made some other friends conspicuous by their absence. Like most of my rehabilitation, it was down to just me again. I could either start afresh and get back into circulation or sit in a comfortable chair and rot, which is the easy way out. The first option was the obvious choice for me and after a short while some confidence did eventually return – so much so, in fact, that I agreed to meet some friends at the local bar to sink a few orange juices. Alcohol was no longer an option. Both times I had suffered a seizure the first question asked by my doctor was, 'Had you had a drink?' So I chose to refrain, purely as a means of eradicating as many of the risks as I possibly could. It seemed obvious to simply stop drinking alcohol altogether. That night in the bar was a pleasant change. It felt good to be circulating again and it was smiles all round as the evening progressed. Slap!

Headache, hallucinations, a loudly yelled, 'Get me out of here,' and for the third time I was waking up back at home with a migraine. The medication I had been put on obviously wasn't working, so hello square one again. The frustration was overwhelming to find I had wasted my time taking medication. On that occasion the seizure had been a serious one and I felt as ill as I had ever felt since the accident. So much so, that before the week was out I had been admitted into hospital again. I was nearly on first-name terms with everyone who worked there. As I lay in the hospital bed looking around, everything became far too familiar. I was back in the same place I had been admitted to on my return from Germany. Although by then a whole year had passed, I could still remember every minute of my first stay. I hated the place.

One of the few bonuses gained from being in a coma was that I had been unaware of all of the tests that had taken place to find the extent of the damage done. I was soon to discover the pleasures I had missed as the hospital in my own country ran the very same tests all over again, in an effort to discover the cause of the epileptic seizures.

The first test was the easiest – a brain scan, a simple procedure that involves lying on your back and that's it. Unfortunately, if you have even the slightest hint of claustrophobia, it is a very uncomfortable procedure as it involves having your head strapped down securely while being fed into what is quite simply a high-tech X-ray machine, the same shape as a giant toilet roll holder.

After waking from the scan refreshed (boredom rather than drug-induced sleep), the next test was to be a far more trying experience. An EEG measures electrical activity from all the different parts of the brain, while you are undergoing various tasks, none of which involve exercise of any kind. Sounds easy, but not so. The reason for having the tests done, as already mentioned, was to try and establish what was causing the seizures and so the tasks were of the kind that did not make the thirty minute stay very easy. They involved staring into bright flashing lights, intense deep breathing, then opening and closing my eyes whilst still exposed to the lights – conditions that may induce a seizure in certain patients. It was a deliberate attempt to monitor the activity in my brain prior to a seizure occurring, not something I enjoyed or ever wanted to go through again. It seemed as if the intent was to bring on illness, and I had had enough of illness.

The morning of tests finally ended with another syringe of blood being dragged out of my arm. There then followed six days of complete rest that eventually ended with my discharge. I was still taking the same medication that I had been taking on my arrival and apart from one morning of tests, I failed to see the reason why I had been admitted in the first place. I suppose the people who had some prior knowledge of what they were dealing with (and I certainly didn't come into that category) had their reasons. At least I could then go home and try to work out what they were. A more pressing concern, however, was what was to come from my meeting with the final doctor to see me in the hospital.

On being informed of the accident, by that time sixteen months previously, concern and worry were the first emotions that my parents trawled through. Eventually though, more practical considerations came to the fore with the first one being a 'somebody is to blame for this' out-look. A solicitor had been seen, informed of all the details and the process of finding a guilty party had begun. That final doctor to see me before I left for home was a German based in England who had agreed to see me, check me over and report back to the authorities in Germany, rather than having to listen to British reports of my condition. The extent of my injuries and their impact on my life were obviously relevant to any potential claim for damages. A broken arm would most probably have led to the employers concerned handing over a month's wages, shaking my hand and disappearing for ever. Brain damage puts a very different complexion on the proceedings. A sizeable amount of money would be making its way in my direction if liability could be proved.

In any legal case, proving that any party was at fault is the most difficult part of the legal jigsaw. In my own case, I had a trump card. Those photographs taken seconds after the accident by George, showing a German employee hastily erecting safety barriers around the stairwell with my prone body two storeys below could have proved vital. I, along with my legal representation in England and Germany therefore had high hopes of success based almost entirely on one reel of film. Our confidence was short-lived however. The company involved had since gone bankrupt and so any hopes of proceeding with a case against them ended there and then. Yet another slap to an increasingly swollen face! There was however, still a chink of light.

I soon received correspondence from Germany in the form of a letter as a direct result of my meeting and conversation with that German doctor. There was still a chance that I could be entitled to a form of pension that would be paid by the Bauberuffgenossenschaft, the German federation who can provide for victims of accidents. The examination carried out by the doctor had, in actual fact, been a preliminary check by that organisation to establish whether I had a claim. This was very good news – the first for quite some time. However, the letter did end on an ominous note by informing me that there may be a need for me to once again travel to Germany and undergo an extensive set of tests for their own records. Hospital again, in Germany again. Oh fabulous, I can't wait! was not a thought that immediately sprung to mind. Still, it was a long way off. For the present I would put it to the back of my mind and concentrate on conquering the epilepsy and getting back into circulation.

Chapter Ten

The Return

In the months following the accident, George had kept in touch, despite continuing to live and work in Germany. However, the work was never going to last and had finally come to an end. He had decided to return to England to pursue the career he had always wanted to before finances drew him over the water. Anyone in Germany who cared to listen had heard the stories. He wasn't going to be merely an artist, he was going to be the world's premier graphic designer. The time had come to study and study hard. It would no longer be a dream. He would try. And if he failed? Well, at least he had tried. But for George his German tour had not only brought him money but also a serious relationship. The German love of his life would be visiting our country and once more he was in touch, enquiring whether I would hop on a train and travel down to meet her. It would also be our first meeting since his visit to the hospital in Leipzig. It would be good to meet up once again and reminisce about the good and the not so good times.

Travelling for two hours to see a friend was nothing new. I had lived in another country for nine months, for God's sake! The decision to go was easy, however the days leading up to my departure and the journey itself were two of the most difficult things I had ever done. Since the accident I had done nothing alone. Now I had the epilepsy to contend with which made me only feel safe in company, in case anything untoward should happen. Suffering a seizure alone in strange surroundings was a possibility that made me tremendously nervous.

I was learning about my condition with the passing of each seizure and exactly a week before I was due to leave, yet another struck. The customary three days of headaches and general nausea followed. If my past experiences were to repeat themselves, I had got the seizure out of my system and had at least a month to wait before the next one, if indeed there would be a next time.

Safe in the knowledge that I could make the journey and meet up with an old friend, I got on the train. The two-hour trip was completed easily enough, with only occasional bouts of mild panic. I bought a newspaper before departure and read it from front to back in an attempt to concentrate on anything other than the scenery flashing by at a rate of knots – something which may well trigger another epileptic seizure.

George's familiar voice greeted me on the doorstep of his home and suddenly I felt as if my stay in Germany had never ended. George grinned, introduced me to his Fraulein, sat me down and the jokes began. I would be spending the next three days with a good friend who hadn't been around through my rehabilitation, while friends and a fiancée had disappeared and epilepsy had appeared out of the blue. The three days passed quickly with few mentions of sickness and accidents as George had no real knowledge of anything that had occurred since he had called that ambulance back in Leipzig. Although he had constantly been in touch with my family during my stay in hospital and with me ever since, he couldn't fully understand how I was until he had spent some time with me.

Despite that, it was a pleasant change to escape from routine and spend some time away. The return journey seemed just that little bit easier and for the first time in a very long time, I had a smile on my face upon entering my home. It was wiped off my face the very next day. It was slap time again.

The envelope on the floor staring at me and in particular the German stamp looked threatening. The appointment had arrived. I would be going back to Germany for the stringent tests that the last letter had warned me about. Oh joy! My trip to see George seemed a lot easier compared to another trip to Germany. On leaving the country, I had been convinced that I would never even contemplate returning, let alone go back to a hospital!

Those hours I had spent with the psychologist in therapy had seemed a waste of time to me, yet the fruits of his labour were about to become apparent. In the early sessions of therapy, the shrink had decided that it would be more beneficial to me if I was to meet him in a busy shopping arcade. Eventually, that would surely overcome any nervousness I had about being alone. He had mentioned something about 'deep end' and 'throwing'. I had been made to walk all around that arcade once or twice until any nerves and anxiety had vanished completely. When I had finally felt comfortable, he had asked why I had felt so ill at ease in the first place. One reason I gave was the feeling that people were staring at me and being conscious of it. The man with the diplomas then suggested that I jump up and down and wave my arms until everybody would indeed be staring at me. At that point in the proceedings, pride kicked in and pushed all the nerves aside. I said that there was no way I would be making a fool of myself just for his benefit.

I think that that was the turning point that made him and myself realise that I was slowly returning to normality. The trip to see George had also proved that. However, I would be needing all my strength, along with huge amounts of pride to get me through the forthcoming hospital visit with a smile on my face.

Hamburg, Germany – a place of interest and plenty to see. Unfortunately, there was nothing there that could take my mind off the next three days as we passed through the city from the airport on our way to the hospital. The authority in Germany responsible for my being there had decided, generously, to pay my travelling expenses, along with those of a companion of my choice. My good friend, Jim had decided to take full advantage of that opportunity and accompany me on the trip. Our trip from the airport was punctuated by laughing out loud while pointing to advertising hoardings and shop signs that meant something quite different in English. The hospital finally appeared and our taxi followed into the car park, the van of a catering company emblazoned with the owner's name – 'I. WANK'!

Soon after introducing myself at reception, I was being questioned by three specialists and filling small bottles with various bodily fluids, some of them provided naturally and some via a needle. The agenda for the visit was duly explained and it soon became clear that it was going to be no holiday. All of the essential tests, brain scans, X-rays, and an EEG were all to be fitted into my three-day visit. On top of all of those dubious pleasures, I would have to relive the whole experience of the accident, the subsequent weeks in the hospital in Leipzig and undergo a rigorous amount of questioning as all the arrangements had been made for the solicitor working on my case in Germany to meet me in the clinic during my brief visit.

The whole stay flew by at snail's pace but the tests were eventually completed. Jim and myself were forced to escape from the vicinity of the clinic every day and sample German culture as it was his first visit. On the day of departure we were fortunate enough to climb into a taxi that was being driven by a fluent English-speaking German approximately the same age as us, with the same interests and the same sense of humour. He had arrived to collect us in plenty of time and took it upon himself to give us the grand tour of Hamburg, thereby turning our last day into a very enjoyable one. It was a timely reminder of my experiences of German hospitality.

*

I returned to England pleased to have got the whole thing over with, but disappointed at the information that I gleaned from the solicitor. My employers at the time of the accident were indeed bankrupt and there was little point in continuing with the case. The federation set up to help people such as myself would extend a financial helping hand, yet the first small cheque to arrive wasn't nearly enough to take my mind off the fact that somebody, somewhere in Germany, was breathing a huge sigh of relief and failing to give as much as a second thought to my predicament or indeed that of the many others like myself, normal hard-working men who were lured to Germany with promises of huge pay packets and the chance to return home happy; not with broken bones or brain damage, or even in some cases in a wooden box. I was lucky enough to have avoided the final category by the skin of my teeth yet returned a completely different person to the broke, irresponsible man who had set off nine months previously.

The months that followed my departure taught me a lot. Some of the people I knew who called themselves friends had walked away when the going got tough and only the truly loyal remained. The less loyal had proved that they were hardly worth a thought in the first place. It is a shame that it took something so serious for me to see it and yet I'm glad I did. A head injury will only change you if you let it and epilepsy is not something to be frightened or ashamed of and if anyone around you is, be ashamed of them. There is little point in waiting for people to change as they rarely do. Simply move on and get on with your life. You are not here for ever, not even for very long, so don't waste any time and enjoy it while it lasts.

Epilogue

1st June 1997

Announcer: 'The 11.30 flight destined for Leipzig, Germany, is now boarding at gate three.'

The time had come to confront the demons, something about climbing back on to the horse, I was told. Almost three and a half years since I had left the city sitting in that wheelchair, I had decided that it was time to return in order to visit the hospital that my family and close friends knew so well and of which I could only clearly remember those four damn walls. At some point in the trip I would visit the homes of Christian, Romy and Claudia and if time allowed, I would attempt to find that house. I wasn't sure why, I just had to see it. Having a fresh set of memories to replace the old nightmares could only help. I would soon see.

Jim once again climbed further into debt and chose to come along for the ride. A free shuttle would pick us up outside the airport and take us the short distance to one of my many overnight stays during that first arduous tour, the train station right in the centre of Leipzig. Apart from the two trips by train that I had taken with Terry, first to Berlin and then to Magdeburg, one night, just one night, was the sum total of the amount of time that I had spent in the building and yet I could remember every brick. I had later spent nine weeks in a place where four small walls and various people brandishing medical instruments were my only clear memories.

'No problem. I know a nice place where we can buy a cup of coffee and an English newspaper without even leaving the station.'

It was a nice theory, yet a very, very wrong one. Inside the still very impressive building stood nothing at all. My memory was obviously playing tricks with me, but no, three years down the line and Leipzig Hauptbahnhof had finally made it to the head of the refurbishment queue.

Then, '*Andy*,' yelled Christian from the other side of the station and suddenly everything seemed familiar. Christian hadn't changed at all and the smile never left his face throughout our two-day visit.

'It's here somewhere,' I muttered as we strolled around an almost new housing estate containing nothing but very expensive houses when, without warning, I froze. To the right of me outside the front door, an entire family were sitting around a table laughing and joking in the bright sunshine. Only two metres behind that door was the stairwell that three years earlier I had... The happy family will never know who they saw standing rigidly outside their home was. However, they have now taken their place in my memory and nudged to one side those of a deep hole, bare concrete and Glyn's prophetic words – 'Some poor bastard is going to go head first down that one day.'

The last time Claudia had seen me, I had been lying in a hospital bed looking not at all healthy. I was still confused and had absolutely no idea who the strange foreign woman was. Since being discharged from the German hospital and returning to England, I had been told on numerous occasions about how she had helped my family and yet I had no recollection. I knew nothing. Standing outside the door of her home, I was nervous. I was about to meet a woman who knew my close family, who had helped me in the space of nine weeks too many times for a simple 'Thank you' to suffice. I knocked on the door to her home and after a long wait the door swung open, her face lit up, two arms gripped me tightly and for the rest of that night I was part of her family. Although she knew various members of my family well, that was the first time that she had spoken to me when I had been fully aware of who or what was in front of me. As the reunion drew to a close, Claudia picked up the telephone and informed the hospital that I would be visiting the next day. I didn't have to ask – she assumed – and the staff would be waiting for me.

'Intensive care,' I said to the receptionist and my accent brought a smile to her face. She had previously struggled to understand my entire family and now at long last it was my turn. It didn't take her long to understand what I was saying; she didn't have to be a genius to successfully guess my identity. Suddenly nurses appeared, doctors appeared, there was much hugging and handshaking and then, there it stood, *my* bed, as if I had only walked out of the building the day before. Memories that I hadn't been aware of returned and suddenly, just a fragment of those nine weeks was no longer a blur and a tear appeared.

Everything was exactly how I had left it. All the objects that had been my friends for nine weeks were painfully familiar: the table I had eaten all those dubious meals off still stood to one side of the room; the basin that I had sat in front of to wash myself or to be washed by one of the nurses, still stood in one corner of the room; and that commode, well, I didn't even look. Finally, as I had been expecting, those four walls hadn't changed one bit.

The only difference that I could see was that *my* bed was no more and instead it was home to a very frail old lady who was struggling to breathe. The doctor standing beside me still with an arm across my shoulders caught my eye and then shook his head as if to say, 'Not long.' Suddenly I had a new memory of the hospital and it was even more disturbing than the ones I already had. That unfortunate lady would never get the chance to leave the hospital, even in a wheelchair and would never again return home. She would never know how badly her stay in the bed had affected her or if her family and friends would struggle to cope when the euphoria of her survival had passed. And epilepsy? She would avoid that as well. In an instant, memories became unimportant and the luck that I had been so fortunate to have just before Christmas '94, was worth dwelling on more, as the other means of escape from that hospital that I had come so close to did not bear thinking about.

A visit from Romy heralded the final day of our stay and after a brief tour of the area, 'Die Ocean', Seaweed's shop and a look at the holiday unit that I had been just a touch careless with, the trip was over. In two days, I had wandered around Leipzig and nobody in the city I had come into contact with who had been unaware of the reasons for my visit had noticed the problems I had. How could they? I had been walking, I had been talking and there wasn't even a visible mark on my body that hinted at what happened in December '94. If, just for five minutes, one of the population could have seen inside my head, inside my mind, they would have known and yet they never will.

I do not need a wheelchair or twenty-four hour a day care and so am I fit and healthy? Well, no. I just have problems where they can never be seen. I sometimes wish they could, but what difference would it make? To understand a subject, someone has to tell you first and if anybody does know, will they please tell me.

'Every day is a bonus,' people have said to me hundreds – no thousands – of times and I agree, yet every day is a meticulously prearranged day. Where will I rest or even sleep if I have to? Where is the escape route should I feel those telltale tremors in my body? Have I made sure that I have taken *all* of my medication? When is the next migraine going to strike? Will I remember the conversation that I've just been having in the morning or in just five minutes time? And where is the next stairwell, because you can't always see them? Every day is a bonus...? I really and truly do not know.

4th June 1997

I had cleared the final hurdle and not one of the obstacles that my brain could put in the way had stopped me. Yes, I had suffered the occasional headache and the odd epileptic scare, but I was not, however, still lying in my bed with a doctor standing nearby shaking his head as if to say, 'Not long.' And yet it still rings in my ears, Is every day a bonus? Maybe 'bonus' is the wrong word. A lesson? Certainly.

The End?

Not on your life!

Appendix One

THE POSSIBLE OUTCOME OF BRAIN INJURY

Each person who has a brain injury has unique physical, intellectual or social rehabilitation problems

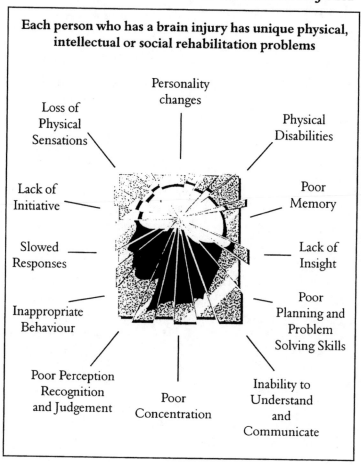

Personality changes

Loss of Physical Sensations

Physical Disabilities

Lack of Initiative

Poor Memory

Slowed Responses

Lack of Insight

Inappropriate Behaviour

Poor Planning and Problem Solving Skills

Poor Perception Recognition and Judgement

Poor Concentration

Inability to Understand and Communicate

Appendix Two

Around 1,000,000
people attend hospital as a result of head injury. Of these:

About 150,000
will have a minor brain injury resulting in unconsciousness for fifteen minutes or less. Many will have short-term loss of attention, concentration and memory. Usually they recover completely within three to six months.

Around 10,000
will suffer moderate brain damage causing unconsciousness for up to six hours. Some will still have physical and psychological problems after five years.

Up to 11,600
will suffer severe brain injuries and be unconscious for six hours or more. Of these, only about 15% will return to work within five years. Many will not work again and around 4,500 will require full-time care for the rest of their lives.

More than 120,000
people in the UK are currently suffering from the long-term effects of severe brain damage caused by head injury. This number is increasing every year.

ALMOST AUF WIEDERSEHEN

Andy Nicholson

MINERVA PRESS

ATLANTA LONDON SYDNEY

ISBN 0 75410 508 3

First Published 1999 by
MINERVA PRESS
315–317 Regent Street
London W1R 7YB

Printed in Great Britain for Minerva Press

ALMOST AUF
WIEDERSEHEN

For the doctors and nurses at Sankt Elisabeth Krankenhaus, Leipzig, for first saving my life and then putting me on the long road to recovery. 'Thank you' is not enough. For the staff at St George's Hospital, Lincoln, for carrying on the good work and for Velma Boulter at the Epilepsy Liaison office in Doncaster for all her help.

Also for my family, Darren, Cookie, Steve, Heather, Christian, Romy, Claudia and everyone else who could be bothered to hang on in there when the going got tough. You know who you all are… and are not.

Special thanks go to Tina for her enthusiasm and to Jo Fereday at Headway, Lincolnshire, for her continued assistance.

Finally, thank you Claire, for a new lease of life.

Foreword

Life was once described to me as a pack of cards and that life's incidents were the jokers. My understanding is that the jokers represent changes in life and we humans don't readily adjust to change. *Almost Auf Wiedersehen*, I feel, gives an insight on how these jokers can be played, and when the chips are down how the unexpected can happen for good or bad.

As someone who helps care for a person with a head injury, I have a certain understanding of how difficult and devastating life can be after a life-threatening incident has occurred. But Andy's writing of *Almost Auf Wiedersehen* has enabled me to gain a new insight into the fear, anger, frustration and constant battles of everyday living. Throughout the journey of this difficult and untimely change in his life, I feel he shows that the beginning of acceptance can only come from within.

Help, support and information, although not always readily available, may assist a person to begin to adjust to change. It is my understanding that only the person themselves is able to begin to understand how this acceptance and change feels.

Thank you 'Andy from Lincoln' for sharing your hopes, thoughts, fears and inspirations and a heartfelt 'well done' for achieving so much in the face of so little encouragement.

Jo Fereday,
Chairman of Lincolnshire Headway

Contents

Chapter One

Work in Germany?
Go on Then!

Life is one long, rocky road. You search for the highs and ride out the lows. Once in a while, someone's journey is interrupted by a solid brick wall blocking their path. Hitting that unexpected obstacle can bring a great deal of hurt that spreads like wildfire to one's friends and family, to whom they are so important. In the blink of an eye, all of those highs and lows no longer seem important. Those afflicted cannot afford to let them be so. They must start again, afresh; they have no choice.

Twenty-four years had passed me by without my ever having an idea of what I planned to do with the years ahead. Meanwhile, as I spent my life drifting from job to job, the circle of friends with whom I had spent my formative years were becoming everything that you hope to be when escaping from your schooling. A career, marriage and children had fallen into everyone's lap, seemingly without a great deal of effort. After spending five years scraping a living on building sites, it wasn't too long before everything that my friends possessed, suddenly ceased to seem quite so important any more. In fact, before too much longer, some of the friends themselves fell into the same category.

Lucy, my ever-present girlfriend, had stood by me and was continually dipping into what appeared to be an endless pot in order to keep me running. The debts were growing larger by the day. Although I refused to see it, something was going to have to happen and quickly. Then – the telephone rang.

'Hi, Andy, it's Terry,' wasn't what I had been expecting to hear. I had worked alongside Terry on numerous sites, but it had been a year since our paths had last crossed and we had never met outside of working hours. Terry was married with a child on the way and needed money more urgently than I did.

The greetings were out of the way quickly and the reason for Terry's call soon became crystal clear.

'Do you want a job?' was a question that hadn't been put to me for quite some time. My ears pricked up as I suddenly became extremely attentive. I hadn't worked for anyone other than myself for a while and the lure of another party filling my pockets on a regular basis made my eyes light up like beacons. I prepared myself for the usual information that would instantly shatter my illusions. It would be a week of tremendously hard work that could possibly lead to something more permanent, an employer's method of off-loading the work that regular staff are not that keen on doing. For the first time that I could remember, that was not the information that I was about to hear. Terry explained that the job in question was to last for at least six months. The idea of guaranteed work for that length of time was an offer I couldn't afford to ignore.

I, along with the rest of the building fraternity, had heard the rumours surrounding the big money being earned in Germany at that time. We had even watched an entire television series dedicated to the subject, so when Terry announced that the work was in Leipzig, Germany, the beacons that were masquerading as my eyeballs began to flash pound signs! Aside from the money, the aforementioned television series had portrayed the experience as almost exclusively humorous with only the occasional downer. We were about to learn the truth and my own 'occasional downer' would be an almost fatal one.

Like the majority of Brits, I did have my grievances with the German nation. My own centred on nothing so trivial as two World Wars; a certain penalty shoot-out was still fresh in my mind! Trailing close behind that annoyance was the image of the stereotypical German citizen. Would they all be aggressive and totally humourless, as they had been portrayed almost since the written word, or would we find just another group of people with whom we could find no fault if we ignored all the stories and found out for ourselves.

Clearly, choosing to take the work in the middle of the old East Germany was not an easy decision to make, certainly not one to make within a minute over the telephone. I desperately needed the money that a long period of work in Germany, or indeed anywhere, would bring. If the rumours were true, there was no way I could go wrong should I choose to work in the 'Fatherland'. The money was good and a year later I would be able to start again with all my debts cleared.

I would discuss the idea with Lucy and inform Terry of my decision the following week. Leaving the country in order to find work had not entered my mind before. I would have preferred to stay at home until something arrived on my doorstep. I had never been one who relished travelling, but this was the opportunity I had been waiting for. In a year's time, I thought, I would be a different person. Indeed I would be, yet not for the reasons I had been hoping for.

'Lucy, I've been offered a job!' was greeted with a huge grin of relief. The grin wasn't to last long upon hearing that I would be leaving for Germany and spending six months over there. It was always going to be a difficult decision because I had no desire to leave the country, even to find work. A quick glance at the bank balance speeded up the decision and after informing Lucy that I should be able to pay back all the money I owed her in a matter of weeks, it was all that I could do to prevent her from shoving me out of the door! My chief moneylender had spoken, and so the decision was made. Not only would I be able to clear my debts, but I would also hopefully be able to save some money and make a fresh start. Saving, so far, had been alien to me.

The next day I made the telephone call to Terry and informed him of the good news. We had exactly one week before our departure and it couldn't go slow enough as far as I was concerned. Needless to say, the seven days passed by at the speed of light, a phenomena that was aided by the huge quantities of alcohol consumed at the various hastily arranged farewell get-togethers.

The day of my departure arrived far too soon and my hangover was shaken off by my nervousness and dislike at the thought of leaving. The last bit of packing was thrown into Lucy's car and off we went. We would be driven to the port by Terry's father and Lucy had decided to say her farewells whilst taking me to Terry's house, where we arrived after yet another lightning fast passage of time.

Five minutes later she had gone and I was sat alongside Terry, heading off to Hull to catch our ferry to Ostend. A shortage of money had made a flight out of the question, so to travel by sea was the only option remaining.

Fifteen minutes after our arrival at the port, we boarded the ferry and walked on to the deck where we stood feeling very pleased with ourselves, discussing our impending good fortune and what we would be spending the huge wad of cash that we were about to earn in Leipzig on.

The ferry set off on its overnight journey and almost immediately it occurred to me that this was the first time I had ever been on a boat in my whole life, at least one that was moving anyway. The waves that I spent a few moments staring at quickly turned into tidal waves of nausea which swept over me. I looked at Terry who stared back and a cure for the sickness was hastily decided upon. Spending the rest of the night at the disco getting pissed out of our little faces seemed sensible as we would then feel as if the floor was rocking anyway. It was, perhaps, not what any doctor would have prescribed under the circumstances, yet it did seem to work. We became drinking buddies with a long-distance lorry driver who made the journey every week and he offered us the other two beds in his cabin. This kindness took less than two seconds to be accepted. After stopping at every vending machine for a cup of coffee, we reached the cabin and fell into bed to dream about the girls we had in no uncertain terms been ogling just moments before.

The wake-up call came first thing in the morning. We crawled from our beds and bade farewell to our new-found friend. The bathroom in the cabin was to provide Terry and myself with our last wash of any kind for a full two days. Two tired and bedraggled specimens of humankind then dragged themselves through to the dining area for breakfast. The same length of time would pass before a proper meal would be devoured again. Had we known these facts at that time, maybe a little less alcohol would have been drunk the previous night to enable us to eat that little bit more without feeling very sick indeed.

An hour passed by and the ferry arrived at the port where we were to disembark and begin phase two of our journey to Leipzig. We would need to make a short trip to the local train station to catch the first train – a short trip which turned out to be two miles. An awful long way on foot when there is a large suitcase to carry each, along with two dirty great tool bags stuffed to the brim with heavy electrical appliances and other hand-held equipment. After an exhausting walk which led to our arms stretching to two inches longer than when we started, we reached the station. Neither one of us had a wallet packed full of money, so Terry had taken the very sensible precaution of calling our agent before our departure to find out exactly how much the fare would be. With this prior knowledge, we confidently proceeded to the ticket counter, behind which sat a very friendly and helpful Belgian. As well as these traits, he also had the ability to communicate with us in our native tongue. A good thing, as being English usually means that we have no desire to speak in anything other than just that and won't even begin to try anything else.

What the nice Belgian did manage to explain to us was not, however, what we wanted to hear. Our agent had been very wrong and we currently had less than half of the fare to get all the way through to Leipzig. Frankfurt was as far as we could reach. We decided to keep going and travel to Frankfurt, drawing up a list of blunt and very heavy implements that we would be inserting into the agent at speed when we finally met.

A change of train in Cologne put us on the train to Frankfurt, feeling very tired indeed. On arrival at Frankfurt it dawned on us that this was the end of the line. It really is a staggeringly lonely feeling standing in a foreign country, tired and hungry without the means to escape. The last remnants of cash in our pockets was used up trying to get hold of the agent or anyone in the world who could contact him for us. All to no avail. The only option left to us was to ask passers-by for money. We decided not to stoop to these depths and instead spent our very last coins on a telephone call each to our loved ones to reassure them that we were all right. I used up my final coin on a call to my parents telling them not to worry at all and that we would arrive okay, while all the time I was absolutely shitting myself. I placed the phone back on its hook and walked out of the booth feeling very depressed. Terry took my place in the booth and also proceeded to lie through his teeth to his wife back in England, who was blissfully unaware of the circumstances that we found ourselves in.

The conversation soon turned to the subject of the expected 'riches' that had been promised to us before our departure from England. The harsh truth was that we could not have been further away from the first cheque. We had made our last telephone calls and we were now without a single penny in our pockets.

As we wandered around Frankfurt train station, we began to feel grateful for the breakfast we had devoured back on the ferry only hours earlier. The chances of eating anything in the near future were looking bleak at best. We had no option other than stooping to the depths that we had only minutes earlier dismissed. I stood guard over our luggage as Terry started to endlessly trawl the station searching for anyone with a kind-looking face, who would believe the yarn he told them, if indeed they understood him in the first place. After an hour of begging, one shiny mark found its way into Terry's palm and we aimed for the nearest telephone, hoping that our one coin would be enough to enable us to contact our agent and get some much needed help.

Amazingly, our luck turned and we at last spoke to the man who wasn't exactly top of our Christmas card lists. He agreed to pay for two tickets with his credit card, via the telephone and we could then climb aboard the very next train to Leipzig. It was then that another problem reared its head. The next train to Leipzig would not be leaving until the following morning. It was then 5 p.m.

At first glance, the platforms in a train station do not appear to be at all comfortable. On second glance, your first impressions prove to be correct. We chose to ignore the platforms and head back into the station itself for warmth and, far more importantly, the armed guards in the station made us feel safe, while at the same time filling us with dread as our minds imagined all the different reasons why they were there in the first place.

One of the less frightening aspects of the station also proved to be one of the most alarming. Our run of luck, that had turned for the better on speaking to the agent, swung full circle as it became apparent that unfortunately we had strayed into what appeared to us to be the homosexual capital of Europe! In the space of two hours it was pointed out to me on numerous occasions what an 'incredibly attractive sexpot' I was, unfortunately by the wrong gender for my tastes. I could have made more money in one evening inside Frankfurt train station than I was to manage in the whole duration of my stay in Germany!

Eventually, we discovered a place to sit and rest, almost out of sight of the homosexual jamboree that was to take place through the night. To add to our discomfort, the station was also home to a large gathering of alcoholics and drug users who themselves were desperately trying to avoid the beggars, a category which we were fitting into. Needless to say, that part of ex-Soviet-ruled East Germany was not the best introduction to its people and their heritage and it certainly was not going to provide us with a good night's sleep. On the two occasions that our eyes did at last close, a jab in the ribs from the barrel of a security guard's rifle was a swift reminder of the danger of sleeping and not being alert to the petty thieves.

Morning arrived. The twenty-four hours since our arrival had felt like an entire week. The train could not depart fast enough, and I never wanted to see Frankfurt again as long as I lived. A look at the timetable hanging between the graffiti on the walls told us that our train would be leaving from Gleis Drei. A minute passed as we attempted to translate the meaning of the words, when a quick look at one of the many platforms told us that it meant Platform 3, and so we waited excitedly on one of the many benches that we had chosen not to sleep on during the night. Ten minutes late, five sizeable rubbish containers sitting precariously on wheels, masquerading as a train, pulled up to the platform, and we boarded. We could sit quietly for two hours in comfort. It was to be our third train journey in twenty-four hours, but this one was different. This was the train to riches! Ignorance is bliss.

The train wove its way through East Germany for what felt to us like a week. After spending a night in a Western train station and previously travelling through the country's cities and surrounding countryside, the difference in the view from the train that we then had was astonishing. From pristine cleanliness and vulgar opulence to the sights of a harsh and bleak way of life in the space of thirty minutes. The contrast was almost unbelievable. Back in Frankfurt station, all we had needed to do was step outside to find ourselves in the middle of all the normal trappings of a large Western city – vast shopping arcades, restaurants, expensive accommodation and nightclubs adorned with yards of neon lighting. The fact was that we were now in the East which had a long way to go to match the excesses of its Western counterpart.

Staring out of the window, it was obvious that there were few new buildings to be seen, or at least ones that looked new to us. There were however, hundreds of building sites to be seen and it was clear that if we were to journey on the same route ten years later, the view would be very, very different. We could see that communism had given everyone a home, but in true Red style, they all appeared identical. Rows of huge blocks of apartments signalled our entrance into a town or city. On the positive side, it seemed that shortly after that monumental day when the Wall had finally fallen, the authorities had decided that the advancement of the country and the changes it would bring would not happen slowly. Everything had started immediately.

Springing from the ground everywhere, it seemed, were vast housing estates, factories with familiar Western names and business parks containing the office blocks that gave off the aura of a wealthy nation. Leading from all that new-found freedom were the hundreds of miles of brand new roads that were under construction. It is all well and good having the trappings of success, but you still have to be able to reach them. So at the same rate as the buildings were rising up, the roads were being laid down. No matter where the train was on its journey to Leipzig, we could always see at least one gang of road builders attempting to get their particular stretch of road finished almost before they had started, and there was never ever a time when at least one crane could not be seen. It was as if, even when a toilet was installed, a crane was needed.

The whole eastern side of the country was a mirror image of our own country. Back in England are miles of countryside dotted with towns and building sites. The journey we were taking was revealing mile upon mile of sites, and occasionally we would arrive at a small patch of greenery. As quickly as we had entered it, we were out again and in the shadow of yet another crane. We had almost worked out when to expect each patch of greenery when we finally arrived in Leipzig, journey's end.

The outskirts of the city were much the same as the entire scene preceding them, yet the station we finally pulled into was spectacular. The largest 'end of line' train station in Europe welcomed two expectant Englishmen, eager to get a slice of the work they had spent the previous three hours looking at. Any reservations we had been carrying with us were dispelled after we saw for ourselves this sheer volume of work awaiting us. It was difficult to believe the work would only last six months – the next decade seemed a more realistic estimate.

Happily, the first voices we heard on disembarking from the train were those of two Englishmen, Tom and Keith who had been sent to meet us. A sight for sore eyes if ever there was one – the first genuinely friendly English-speaking people we had met since bidding farewell to the lorry driver back on the ferry. We were, however, about to receive the first in a very long line of slaps in the face. Our agent who had given us the chance to work in Germany had left for a break in England the very same day and left no money at all for us to make our arrival more comfortable.

Tom and Keith had been working in the area for some time and were living in a complex of holiday homes a short distance away from the station. Tom had been told of our impending arrival and had booked us into the bungalow next to his own, a bungalow consisting of a bedroom, a bathroom and a small area for cooking. Not much but adequate nonetheless. After a short journey, we arrived and Tom set about feeding us the entire contents of his fridge – two egg sandwiches. We thanked Tom for his generosity and vanished next door to our own digs, where we settled in to enjoy eight sensational hours of sleep.

Chapter Two

We're Really Cooking Now

The morning after our arrival, Tom showed us to our place of work via the surprisingly efficient network of trams that Leipzig boasts – free if we pretended not to understand that a ticket was required. After the first in a long series of tram joyriding expeditions we reached our workplace – a four-storey building that was to be the brand new local headquarters of a German telephone company. It didn't take a genius to work out that the East German telephone system had to quickly go the same way as the rest of the region and expand. In a very short space of time, Germany was preparing to become the powerful united nation it had once been.

The views of the vast majority of the English workers out there at the time was that they couldn't really care less what the newly reunited country was going to metamorphose into, just so long as a pile of money appeared in their wallets every weekend. The more patriotic, or perhaps more foolish amongst us, agreed that eventually we would end up flattening it all over again and our grandchildren would be standing in the same spot in years to come discussing yet another rebuilding programme. I hoped that tongues were stuck firmly in cheeks on making those rash judgements and of course they were – I think.

With the sightseeing over, Tom led us into the building and up to where we would be working. Up and up and up.

Only four floors, but still carrying the two heavy bags of tools that were now part of us, it felt like scaling Mount Everest. On reaching our area of work we soon discovered that there was going to be nowhere safe to leave the tools overnight. That problem was soon remedied by removing part of a plasterboard wall that appeared solid to the untrained eye. The hole would serve as a safe unless we were observed hiding the gear. If that happened, it was a certainty that the 'safe' would be empty the following morning.

Midway through our safe-making exercise, Terry suddenly let out an ear-piercing yelp as three strangers to me appeared on the other side of the room. It transpired that Terry's yelp had consisted of the two words 'small world'. Incredibly, the three men walking towards us had previously worked with Terry back in England. Out of all of the building sites that were employing people at that time, we had walked on to one that three of Terry's former workmates were working on – 'small world' indeed! After much back-slapping, we told them the whole sorry story of our night in the train station and of our agent's inability to discover the true cost of train fares. When they and the rest of the men around began to nod repetitively at our every word, it was obvious that they had heard it all before and our confidence in our agent took a nose-dive.

Luckily, prior to his disappearance, the agent had managed to pay our new-found friends, who on observing our empty pockets, reached into theirs and lent us enough money to at least feed ourselves for the next two days. We promptly removed anything unsightly off their boots with our tongues and went to find the nearest café and fill our painfully empty stomachs. With the trauma of arriving with no money over, we were about to receive another slap in the face though.

You usually find that when you are working in another country, you and your fellow countrymen stick together in the first few days as you tend not to mix with the strange-talking people that you see. You tend to rely very heavily on your mates as initially there is no one else, and so you have no choice. Every work break our little circle of expats would get together and discuss money, women, football and home. The first time we joined in one of those friendly gatherings, we wanted to learn about the pay system we had yet to experience. It turned out to be very different from what had been explained to Terry back in England in the comfort of his own home. After replying to our agent's advertisement in our local newspaper, a lengthy telephone conversation had taken place in which Terry had tried to glean as much information as he possibly could. Our agent had quoted all of the prices for every aspect of the work that we were to be doing. However, his information had fallen into the same bracket as the one including the cost of our train fares and it was entitled 'Blatant Lies'. Not only had he exaggerated the prices, but he had also failed to tell Terry about his own slice of the pie and a large slice it was too. He was, after all, only a middle-man standing between his employees and a large German building company and Terry had failed to check the verbal small print. After the unexpected deductions had been made, we would be earning approximately half of what we had been expecting. We had already expected a twelve-hour day, but any more seemed impossible and so our confidence took another huge knock as this second slap in the face struck us.

A tentative first day of work was completed and we followed Tom out of the building and on to the tram destined for our bungalows. The conversation revolved around finding something slightly more painful than the array of carpentry utensils we possessed to insert into the agent at speed when we finally got to meet him. Sharp was easy –

we wanted something blunt to add to his pain, like a baseball bat, a scaffold pole, or an articulated lorry! We had a week to discover the most painful article. In the meantime, living took priority. We had eaten on that first day at work due to the generosity of Terry's colleagues, but it was the rest of the tour that was worrying us. We couldn't continue to scrounge off our workmates, so we looked for some cheap food – not such a difficult task wherever you are as there's always bread and water. We soon found cheap meat to add to those two basics and so at every mealtime for the next four days the only solids to pass our lips aside from the bread, were eggs and spicy German beefburgers known as Frikadelle. These particular items of German cuisine were extremely tasty, yet we lived in constant fear that the Frikadelle could possibly evolve into living creatures overnight as the smell they carried with them could only have been made by something living. We were certainly not prepared to take the chance many of the natives did, of eating them uncooked. The largest saucepan in the bungalow was filled to the brim with cooking oil and heated to supernova. It was only then that the dubious foodstuff would be eaten after at least ten minutes of cooking in boiling oil to be absolutely positive that there was nothing alive on our plates.

With the culinary delights over, then would come an empty period of time as it became apparent that without money there was nothing at all to do but watch German television programmes. When you are bored every night without fail, it really is amazing just how much you think you are understanding whilst staring blankly at a television screen. The storylines that we made up were undoubtedly better than the real ones, but there was no way that they could have been shown at peak time. Childish? Yes, indeed, but you have to pass the time somehow. Luckily there wasn't a great deal of time to kill as it soon became an understanding that at approximately 8 or 9 p.m. every night, Tom and Keith would arrive weighed down with a crate of beer, a cheap yet lethal brew that made whiling away the hours so much more fun. We would sit and talk, getting to know one another and attempting to have a laugh to make the time pass more quickly.

The first weekend in Germany started with a Saturday spent on the site trying to earn the much sought-after pile of banknotes. Sunday followed, our only day of rest. As we were new to the area, sitting inside all day staring out of the window was not a good idea. We had to get out and find our way around for future reference. We were not destined to travel too far from home on our initial weekend as Tom and Keith decided that we should be introduced to the rest of the park we were living on and so we took the full guided tour.

We had a half-mile walk to cover before our first destination was reached. The only sights to be seen were drinking establishments to the left and drinking establishments to the right. The German love of beer had found a home in the middle of the park, it seemed. It would have been discourteous of us to walk past them all, so one, two or possibly eight pit stops were made before our journey was completed.

Right in the middle of the acres of greenery was a huge man-made beach laid around a scenic lake. There were hundreds of visitors to the area including almost every British worker living in the area. We had no idea as to why this was their chosen spot until a glance at the beach revealed everybody, quite literally! Yes, every Sunday the place where we lived turned into a cross between heaven and a scene from a *Carry On* film. Hundreds of Brits wearing shorts and T-shirts were surrounded by nothing but naked flesh.

Sunglasses were the order of the day, not to protect our eyes but to hide behind when ogling any particular beauty who took our eye. Good old-fashioned British prudishness was making it extremely obvious who the foreigners were; any sign of clothing gave away our presence. Shame had long vanished when we all set about trying to find the young attractive bodies floating in a sea of aged whales.

One of our confident colleagues stripped down to a very slinky thong and joined the natives basking in the heat. A harmless venture, yet when surrounded by slightly inebriated friends, it was a move always destined to end in humiliation. Sure enough, his workmates joined us in a bar to give their friend time to doze off. After a short wait they returned to where he was basking and they very gently removed his thong, exposing his nether regions to the ninety-degree heat. The next move was to leave the scene, waving at the numerous chuckling Germans and returning to us to be greeted by a hero's welcome.

The unfortunate target of their joke returned bolt upright and wincing painfully three hours later to much laughter and many denials of guilt. Work for him was to be an uncomfortable exercise for the next few days.

With the laddish fun done with, the day was nearly over with just time to consume one more Frikadelle before catching some sleep. Every head looked towards the beach as we passed by, to avert our eyes from the shameless German men strolling along naked, Bratwurst flapping in the wind! After what should have been a five-minute walk back to the digs had turned into a boisterous sing-along, we split up and headed back towards our respective abodes.

As soon as we reached our bungalow our home-made deep-fat fryer was placed on the heat and we sat back and waited for it to reach its usual murderous temperature. We had become so used to slinging our food rations into the pan that I realised that at no time had we had the opportunity to examine the ingredients within the mock burgers. We had already bought a vast amount of this culinary delight, based purely on appearance alone. Why not? They were cheap, easy to cook and almost pleasant to eat. On that first Sunday, however, I chose to take the bull by the horns and attempt to read the list of ingredients on the side of the packet.

The size of the list made it clear there was far more contained within that solid exterior than meat alone, if indeed there was any meat there in the first place. Once again, the language barrier intervened, with my English to German dictionary being hastily removed from my baggage. This was a handy oracle when we wished to know what a single word meant, but totally useless when trying to translate an entire sentence as in any language there are always certain words which mean one thing if used on their own but something completely different if part of a sentence. The game we had played while watching television, of making up our own storylines, evolved in a slightly different form as our translation of the ingredients got under way. Out of the whole list of words, the only one successfully translated was 'pork'. Therefore, I could only deduce that real pork was probably the only part of the pig that had not been involved in the preparation of our dinner.

Our evening began with a couple of 'trotter burgers'. I had cunningly decided to mask part of the taste by placing slices of cheap cheese on top of them which made our meal almost edible. The evening then took an upturn as an old episode of a popular British soap opera appeared on our television screen. Was this the German way of mastering the English language? Alas, no! As the dubbing started we prepared ourselves to rack our brains and remember what Jack was saying to Vera outside the pigeon loft. We failed dismally, cracked open another bottle of beer and bored ourselves stupid playing cards, or even more sadly, dominoes.

Then out of the blue my memory said, 'Hello', and I suddenly remembered that as I had left England I had packed a personal stereo in the unlikely event that I may need it. A rectangular piece of plastic and two headphones from that moment on became my very best friends and they were to stay with me for so long that I thought I may need to have them surgically removed on my return home to England.

More than one song on my chosen cassette was to remind me of home and bring on an urge to fly straight back at the first available opportunity. One quick look at my empty wallet though and the urge soon died! There was no point in pining for home; we had to get on with our work and wait for our first break from it all in the not-too-distant future. Terry and myself had always agreed that we would work hard for a month and then return home for a week, continuing that routine until we were not needed any more.

Our thoughts at that time turned instead to the imminent arrival of the agent bringing with him our first pay packet, with which we could return the money that had been lent to us on that first day and enable us to look after ourselves rather than relying on our colleagues. Hopefully, we might even be able to send some money back to our loved ones. We were under no illusions that our first princely sum would only cover the bare essentials and that it would be the weeks to follow that produced the goods. We had put down our roots, we had somewhere to live, we had a job and the money would soon be heading our way. Once more – ignorance is bliss!

Our introductory days on the site had simply been a case of being told what we had to do, then reaching into the home-made safe, dragging out our tool bags and getting on with as much work as we possibly could in a vain attempt to earn somewhere near the anticipated wage that we had travelled over for. Every time any work was completed, we had to make sure that every inch of it was meticulously measured and jotted down into our own personal note-books. It may have been necessary to produce these should our agent arrive with a different set of figures. This was a scenario that we had half-expected, so a certain amount of bartering had to be rehearsed. All of the lads on the site who were employed by the same agent were in the same boat. Any disagreements about our pay would be much easier to sway in our favour because of the number of us involved and, unless 'Mr Elusive' arrived carrying a shotgun or with bodyguards in tow, he would surely have to back down to a certain extent to keep his troops happy. After all, while we were working, his pockets would be filled as he took his slice out of our wages. There would be no point at all in angering us all as he would lose out if we were to take offence and down tools.

The day prior to the prodigal son's arrival, the workers gathered during every break to discuss what our limit would be should it come to us being offered much less than we had actually earned. The subject of taking him to one side and talking fairly and logically to him and finally reaching an agreement was discussed briefly, forgotten, and instead violent threats were the favoured suggestion of the day.

With that angle of attack getting a unanimous vote, the usual silliness returned. Much joke-telling and pointless chit-chat replaced the underlying annoyance of our previous debate. Although our conversations swung backwards and forwards from meaningful to pathetic, they proved useful as they were a highly successful method of focusing anyone's attention one hundred per cent on either the problems they had or on simply trying to make everyone laugh, thereby keeping any thoughts of homesickness firmly locked in the backs of their minds for a while. It was difficult enough trying to earn the riches promised, without being depressed and slowing down while you felt sorry for yourself.

On that particular day, we had another reason to take our thoughts off home as our happy gathering was to welcome another worker into its fold. Our agent had suckered another unfortunate individual into filling a travel bag and coming over to join us. An uneventful day's work was half-over when in strolled Lee, upfront, cheery, and all in all an instantly likeable bloke. With Terry and I sleeping two to a three-bed home, it had already been decided that it would be us to look after the newcomer by moving him into our temporary home. It was apparent early on that Lee would be the perfect flatmate, a judgement based almost entirely on the fact that he had been sensible enough to bring over some money to help him in case of an emergency; he wouldn't have long to wait. He came in useful within an hour of his arrival, as after being introduced to Terry and myself, he knuckled down and helped us through the rest of the day's work – an instant friend.

Terry and myself had been in Germany for almost a week and could already be classed as veterans. That gave us the right to discuss with Lee the pitfalls and the lies he had undoubtedly been told in order to get him over to Germany in the first place.

On the now familiar tram ride home Lee added his small collection of hand tools to the growing list of utensils that were to be inserted, etc. The tram was packed as Tom had seen fit to invite all the Brits on our site to a welcome party for Lee – a good excuse for yet another piss-up! It hadn't taken much persuading for all to agree with the need for alcohol and off we all went. Every one of us tried our very best to make Lee feel welcome. We hadn't really needed to bother. From the moment he had walked on to the site and exchanged greetings with everyone, Lee had proved to be very, very easy to get on with and he looked to be enjoying the experience. We had all become mates in the space of one afternoon. The laughter on the ride back to our digs was only punctuated by pauses for breath as Lee constantly broke into song, various classics sung at the top of his voice in a thick Yorkshire accent.

Lee had successfully given every Englishman a bad name by the time we reached our destination and alighted from the tram to huge sighs of relief, some coming from his new workmates, but mostly from the Germans sat cowering at the other end of the vehicle. We were seriously beginning to doubt our ability to cope with Lee full-time if his excitable behaviour continued. He hadn't even had a drink, yet he seemed more intoxicated than the rest of us.

After the short walk home, we threw Lee's belongings into our unit and Terry led him off to join the others back at Tom's next door to get Lee's welcome party up and running. I volunteered to stay behind for a moment or two to make a start on the meal we had been craving for hours. Three Frikadelle and a hastily chopped potato were slung into our already very worn makeshift deep-fat fryer and left to simmer on a low heat while I joined the gathering myself.

Either we had bought a half-empty crate of beer or everyone had been incredibly thirsty as by the time I arrived five minutes after the others, the first bottles were already empty. It wasn't too long before an unopened bottle was winging its way across the room in my direction. Everybody retired outside to the patio as breathing became increasingly difficult due to the thick smog being caused by all the smokers, Terry being the only non-smoker. Lee had arrived laden with duty-free cigarettes which vanished exceedingly quickly, making Terry's life a misery.

Occasionally, when you become involved in conversation under the influence of alcohol, you wander into shock territory as you desperately try to out-disgust each other with tales of broken bones, horrific accidents and other pleasantries. Once Keith had finished telling his story, there was no need for anyone else to try. Since our arrival, we had been wondering just how he had received the truly terrible burns on his left leg that we could not help but look at. You are always afraid to ask anyone to describe any misfortune they may have suffered, but the combination of alcohol and Keith not giving a damn what anybody thought brought the story spilling out.

As a child, he had been involved in a serious car accident and the ensuing fire had left him scarred for life from a very young age. It was definitely not the best story to hear before dinner. Shit, I'm lucky, I remember thinking as I sat listening to Keith's tale of woe. Any thoughts I had had about relating my story of breaking my arm at seven years old were immediately abandoned and instead the talk turned to the issue of our fast-diminishing supply of beer. Ignorance is bliss. If I ever meet the man again, unfortunately I can now rival his story and people will feel sorry for me instead. As Keith said at the time, 'Don't feel sorry for me but treat me as if you know nothing.' Wise words, indeed.

Keith stood up on his scarred leg in a bid to show how agile he still was and made his way to the nearest shop with Lee to fetch more supplies, returning twenty minutes later with a fresh crate for us all to enjoy. Dinner could wait a little longer... Bad move!

The conversation soon turned to laughter as Lee entertained us with a list of very old jokes. It was obvious that in only five hours he had become part of the 'family'. With a new man amongst us, it was inevitable that the conversation would soon turn to the topic of our agent. Lee was forced to sit and listen, yet again, to the full story of our arduous trip to Leipzig. We had already told him once back on the site, but a second airing, along with numerous stories from the other lads about such things as not being paid, being paid late and then back to not being paid at all again, started to make Lee question his decision to travel over. When the subject of what we would be doing to the agent on his eventual arrival with that list of blunt instruments was exhausted, it was time to head off back to our respective abodes and throw some solid food down our throats – hunger had set in. Lee had not eaten since arriving and his luggage was still simply thrown in the corner of one of our rooms. It was time for him to unpack and for all of us to attempt to cook a decent meal.

As Terry, Lee and myself walked to our unit, I remember taking a look through the window and noticing how incredibly dark it seemed inside. I was sure I had left a light on. It really does sound so stupid in hindsight to be stood outside in bright sunshine and eighty degrees heat and trying to work out why it was pitch black inside. Upon opening the door, the mystery was cleared up in a nanosecond. We were greeted by clouds of thick black smoke pouring out of the doorway and, without a second thought, the three of us ran into the unit to discover I had totally forgotten about those three Frikadelle that I had thrown into the pan about two hours previously. Unfortunately neither the cooker nor the fryer standing on it had forgotten!

By the time we arrived on the scene, our dinner was just a touch overdone, as indeed were the curtains and anything flammable in the building! In an instant, blind panic took over as we grabbed our possessions and threw them outside as quickly as possible. We were lucky. Fire feeds off oxygen and as I was only in there for a minute, all the windows were still closed. By shutting the door on my way back to the party I had unwittingly saved all of our possessions, although that was about all I had saved. It was at this moment that Lee uttered a line that will stay with me forever and raised a laugh at the time, despite the seriousness of the situation. 'I expected a warm welcome but this is fucking ridiculous!'

After the panic had died down, we took a proper look around. Although none of our clothes had been burnt, everything was terribly smoke-damaged. For the next few days, it would be blindingly obvious whose digs had been burned.

Tom was kind enough to take us all back to his place once more to sleep on the floor and Lee's first day was turning out to be a bit of an adventure. He didn't seem too bothered though as he and Keith went off to find the nearest tavern. Those who remained tried to make the best out of a tricky situation, but there was no way that I could raise a smile that evening.

As I lay awake that night, I had never been so worried in my entire life. If I would have to pay for the damage, I may as well have given in there and then and done a runner. There was no way I was going to work in Germany for nothing when, after all, had the efficient bastards put in a smoke alarm in the first place, it would have gone off and alerted us to the situation before things got out of hand. My thoughts turned to our agent, who four hours earlier I had wanted to stab with everything I could lay my hands on. Now I just wanted him to get here quickly and sort it all out. If needs be, outright grovelling was on the cards.

I can't really say I woke in the morning, because I'm not sure that I slept at all. When everyone around me started to show signs of life I wandered off next door to have a look at the damage with a clear head, just to see if I had in fact slept and dreamt the whole incident. I hadn't!

I returned and informed the rest of the lads of the carnage next door. We discussed the incident over yet another Frikadelle, something that I had temporarily lost the taste for. Tom explained to us that both of the units had been booked using his name and so it would be he who would venture into the manager's office to pass on the bad news. Terry and I decided to miss work that day and attempt to clear up. To the Germans we would at least appear to be helping.

The rest of the lads made their way to work, leaving Terry and myself to walk next door and begin a long day of cleaning. At first glance, it would surely take more than a single day of cleaning as we observed the battleship grey appearance of, well, everything. The fire had burned itself out before spreading much further than the kitchen. However, the heat inside the building must have been intense and anything that could have melted, had melted. The curtains were just blobs of molten material under the cracked windows. The only evidence of electrical sockets were lines of white molten plastic that had run down the walls and formed yet more unsightly blobs on the floor. Bedlinen that hadn't melted completely looked like fishing nets.

We assessed the situation and decided upon what was a ridiculous plan. We really did believe that by the end of the day nobody would ever know what had actually happened, because we were armed with two flannels and a bucket of soapy water! It was always going to take a little more than that to shift the mess that the fire had left, but we set about it anyway, completely confident. Everything that could be moved was placed outside the unit and the floor was the first thing to receive the flannel treatment. That was easy, one wipe revealing a spotlessly clean floor. The wallpaper was next on the agenda and that proved to be slightly more difficult.

I embarked upon the first of numerous trips to the cigarette machine around the corner, as a means of escape. It was the first time that I had been by myself since we had arrived in Germany. All of a sudden, I felt quite alone after the events of the previous night. I was extremely concerned about what the outcome of my carelessness would be. After all, I was in a foreign country with just enough money to buy cigarettes, I knew few people and had totally ruined a holiday unit, all but burning the thing down. After a slow walk, I arrived back at the shell to the comical sight of Terry holding his little soapy flannel and scrubbing away at the wallpaper with all his strength. The difference his efforts made to the general look of the place was nil. I grabbed the second flannel and got to work. It must have been a sight, watching two grown men, with a cloth the size of a sock, scrubbing battleship-grey wallpaper and no matter how hard they tried, getting nowhere fast. In fact, by the time the soapy water had mixed with the smoke and run down the wall, they looked worse than they had originally!

There wasn't a great deal of laughter that afternoon. We didn't think it was possible for anything to happen that would make us smile, let alone fall about laughing. As usual, just when you aren't expecting it, something occurs that proves you wrong. Two German holidaymakers had been watching the dumb Englanders cleaning the unit and we had noticed them looking at us and acting as if they were going to come over and give us a hand, after they had worked out what to say in English. Either that, or they were having a damned good laugh at our expense. Eventually they finalised a script and headed in our direction. The words that they had spent so long rehearsing were not English that we understood and so the natural progression was charades once more. A game of badminton was mimed while they pointed furiously at our unit. 'Piss off, we're busy,' wasn't in my German vocabulary at that time, but luckily Terry remembered finding a shuttlecock and two rackets on top of a cupboard when we arrived. Terry realised that it was a cupboard that had escaped damage in the fire and so we both nodded to the holidaymakers and Terry vanished into the unit to find the gear and pass it on to them to aid Anglo–German relations.

Basic science for five-year-olds – Lesson One. Heat rises. As far as we could see immediately after diving into the place to rescue our luggage, nothing outside of the cooking area had been damaged in any other way than its new smoke colour scheme. Unfortunately, we had forgotten to check for damage to any part of the unit above eye level. We had obviously not been paying attention to our science lessons as five-year-olds. As we had been sitting next door with all the lads enjoying ourselves, the fire had been slowly getting hotter and hotter until a surge of red-hot air had hit the ceiling and moved quietly and destructively across the building until the oxygen ran out and it could go no further. The curtains at the window had been incinerated but their plastic hooks had been just high enough to avoid the wave of heat. Everything above that height would surely have survived as there was nothing in the building above that point. Nothing at all except for the badminton equipment that Terry had noticed on top of the cupboard the day before.

We saw no reason to upset the Germans, so pretending that nothing had happened, we offered them two headless rackets and a shuttlecock the size of a fruit fly. Not excited at the prospect of playing a game with two sticks and a plastic insect, the Germans left us sitting on the grass, staring at the molten sports equipment next to us and crying with laughter.

It only took twenty minutes for reality to hit home again. Between us we decided that the wallpaper was a lost cause with only flannels to attack it with, and so next on our list of priorities was the furniture. If we could get all of that clean, then at least the bill that would no doubt be presented to me would be a bit smaller. It would be easy. It was only smoke on varnished furniture. It would wipe straight off, or so we thought. We were, however, about to embark upon one of the hardest days of work during our stay in Germany.

Halfway through wiping away the sweat while cleaning one of the greyer chairs, there was a loud knock on the door. As I strolled over to answer the continued banging, I was fully expecting to open up and discover that the two potential badminton players had decided to tell all their friends in the area of our misfortune and invite them over for a good laugh at the dumb Englanders. By that time I was well past caring and prepared myself to stand outside and laugh along with them.

The door opened and in walked one solitary man, approximately the size of two rather large men. One look at the menacing expression on his face told me that he was most definitely not there to have a laugh. Before the 'Come' of 'Come in' had left my lips, he was already inside and having a thorough look around. No greetings, no introduction, he just walked in as if he owned the place. Well, funny that. His brief tour of the unit came to a quick end and with that he stood bolt upright in the middle of the room and continued to survey the damage. While that was happening, Terry and I sat staring at one another, shrugging our shoulders and trying to work out who the hell the intruder was.

The examination of the damage carried on with the deathly silence broken only by loud 'Tuts' every time a badly damaged article was spotted. After fifty 'Tuts' he at last plopped his over-large frame on to one of the less damaged chairs. In the space of five minutes he had successfully managed to frighten us to death with his 'next it's the gallows' demeanour and for all we knew, he was quite probably just another holidaymaker.

The stranger turned out to have a grasp of English that was wide enough to accommodate the word 'manager'. With the truth finally out, I sat myself down across the room and prepared for the worst. I had no idea what was to become of the place. Would he expect me to pay for all of the repairs? Was the place insured for just that sort of accident? Were we going to be homeless? Before his questioning began he was kind enough to make us feel even more ill at ease by alternating his glare between Terry and myself and tutting as if we had deliberately tried to burn the place down and that he had already informed the Polizei. I was just a tiny bit concerned by the fact that I was twenty-four years old and wanted my mummy!

After unintentionally scaring the shit out of us, the inquisition began and our initial impressions proved to be false. We had no need to worry as Herr whatever his name was gave us no reason to believe that our fears of him being judge, jury and executioner had any basis at all. Once his angry looks at the building and at us had ceased, he settled back in order to listen to my account of the events of the previous evening and proved to be not the ogre that we had expected.

When events are fresh in your mind, it is exceptionally easy to give a very clear account of them, always assuming that the person listening to your tales understands what you are talking about. The man seated opposite me with the notepad seemed to have a good understanding of what I had been saying until we had progressed beyond shaking hands and saying hello! Our version of how the fire started was to make its way across the room in part-English, part-German and, most importantly, in the form of yet another bout of charades. Charades being a simple enough method of communication, no matter how much difficulty the person opposite you is having, eventually success is inevitable. Unfortunately, after my well-rehearsed playlet involving turning on a gas stove, sitting looking at my watch and then running for my life, it seemed that my performance was wasted. I could have stood all day doing an Oscar-winning performance for my audience of one and whatever he chose to shout out would be in a different language and impossible for me to grasp whether he was right or wrong. My mime ended after ten minutes in a blur of frustrated arm movements. The nice man wrote in his notepad, quite probably that he had no idea how the fire had started, but that it was almost certainly caused by the carelessness of an insane Englishman who couldn't keep his arms still!

With the cause of the fire still unexplained to our questioner, I decided to start the next part of the discussion myself. 'Is the building insured?' I asked. Now this was understood without the need for any bodily movement. Insurance is an internationally understood word. I breathed a little easier at his willingness to discuss the subject. However, I was not prepared for his response.

'Why, aren't you?' knocked me sideways. Terry gave me a look of horror as we tried to fathom out exactly what was meant by his unexpected question.

Germany has a totally different approach to health and safety to Britain. During any stay in the country you will notice the efficient way everything is done, and insurance is no different. The gentleman started to explain to his disbelieving pupils that everyone in Germany has cover for situations such as the one we found ourselves in. It made a lot of sense that our own personal interrogator would take it for granted that I would have some similar sort of cover to protect myself against the highly unlikely event of me being stupid enough to set a building on fire. He was wrong, and I *was* stupid!

Another five minutes of getting precisely nowhere ended with our visitor not looking quite as perturbed by the events as I had expected. There wasn't a broad grin on his face, yet neither was there a grimace or any suspicion of anger. We had been put at ease by his demeanour and he spent a few minutes questioning us without a hint of aggression. Then he wished to know our names and addresses, something we gave without a second thought. Maybe if he had spent the previous few minutes discussing the situation in an agitated or threatening manner, then perhaps someone else's name would have appeared on his paperwork. He did not ask for any proof at all. A brief look at our passports would have confirmed the information given, if he had been able to read them through the thick covering of soot now covering them. We were quite sure that if we had given two completely false names, however stupid they might have been, they would have been duly noted and off he would have gone, satisfied with our contribution to the discussion. Midway through his chat with the two fantastically honest men standing in front of him, he suddenly rose out of his seat and left the premises, apparently happy with the information we had given to him and with us still having no idea of what was going to happen to either us or the burnt-out shell that we were standing in. If we were to be forced into paying for all of the damage, then the least we could do was continue to fool ourselves into thinking we could repair it ourselves.

After another hour of hard work with our little soapy flannels, Tom, Keith and Lee returned home from the site carrying the obligatory crate of beer, with the intention of forcing some of the contents down my throat to loosen me up and put a smile on my miserable face. Not an easy task, but somebody had to do it.

As the party commenced, it crossed my mind that maybe it was time to inform Lucy of my predicament.

However, I couldn't really tell her anything until I was sure of the outcome myself and so I put off announcing the good news, hoping that she would understand when I finally got round to telling her. 'Honey, I've set fire to a holiday home,' is not the easiest way to start off a conversation. It certainly was not the news that Lucy was waiting to hear back at home! Her money was supposed to start rolling in very soon but the paying for all the repairs would bring that hope to an end for an awfully long time.

The night was spent trying to sleep on the floor of Tom's digs as I ran over the events of our first days on Tour of Duty Number One. We had been in the country for eight days, eaten approximately four good square meals, been able to wash thoroughly on five occasions and I had been totally responsible for turning a much sought-after holiday unit into a large uninhabitable mess. We would never, never look back to the early days of our trip and call them uneventful. I hoped that the remainder of the Germany experience would prove to be a little less stressful, until either the work ran out or we had enough money. It was destined to end for neither of those reasons and one that I had never even considered.

The following morning, Tom chose to tell us that he had been in touch with the agent the day previously and had been informed that 'Mr Elusive' would be arriving a day later than had been scheduled. This change of plan had been caused by the fact that he always travelled to and from Germany in his own motor home. This time he would be picking up another new worker and bringing him along with him. What a kind man, we all thought, until Tom told us that the agent would always charge his passengers slightly more than it was actually costing him to carry them over with him. He certainly never missed a trick, and took every opportunity to line his greedy pockets.

With every titbit of information that we were finding out about the man, the less we were looking forward to his impending arrival. It is very rare that you decide how you feel about a person before you have even met them, yet hatred was not a strong enough word for what I was already feeling towards him. He had already lied about the cost of our journey and allowed us to arrive at the site penniless and having to borrow money from people who, by a million to one chance, we had met before, all because he hadn't been there to give us the advance wages promised in his telephone conversation with Terry. We had been expecting that money to be in our pockets, enabling us to eat, drink and make the expected lengthy telephone calls back home. Our agent's non-arrival had put paid to those plans for at least another day. That list of utensils was growing longer by the minute and by that time, sat proudly at the top of the list was, ironically, his own motor home.

That day at work dragged slower than any day I could remember. We were not looking forward to returning to the unit, being unsure of what we would find there. Our minds were not fully on our work, because we had the very real problem of having nowhere to live.

The jokes were coming at me thick and fast that afternoon. For some strange reason, every English-speaking person within earshot was finding them all extremely amusing, apart from myself. I was letting them all go in one ear and out the other whilst standing and staring at each self-appointed comedian and glaring at them in a 'shut your face' kind of way. My looks of disapproval failed to make any impact though on the gathered masses and so for the rest of the day I was forced to endure every fire quip in the handbook of crap jokes. 'Have you got any smokes?', 'You'll be fired', 'Going out in a blaze of glory?' were just a sample. (However, I would have done exactly the same had I been in their steel toe-capped boots.) Needless to say, the whole day was more than a touch difficult, hitting on painful at times. Once a group of builders get the scent of a joke at someone else's expense, the piss-taking becomes remorseless, lasting for as long as it takes for them to get bored and move on to the next victim. Not unlike school playground behaviour, it is extremely funny if you are giving and not receiving.

What felt like a week passed by as the day's work came to an eventual end. The most exhausting part of the day had involved me hurrying away with a packet of cigarettes to the sanctuary of the nearest available toilet for some richly deserved peace and quiet. Not the most comfortable of places to sit for ten minutes and ponder over the previous twenty-four hours, but for those minutes spent away from everybody's attempts to be funny at my expense, my own toilet was paradise!

By the time we had boarded the tram back to our digs that night, everyone was ready for the rest that the tram seats provided. Having spent a sizeable proportion of the day with my arse parked on a toilet seat, I wasn't quite so pleased with the break. Terry and myself sat surrounded by the same friendly folk who had revelled in making the day as miserable for me as they possibly could and the jocularity continued throughout the forty-minute ride back to base. I didn't care though as I knew for certain that despite the constant hilarity from my associates, the whole fire incident had been a figment of my imagination and when I returned to the scene I would wander around the offending quarters, find nothing amiss and have the last laugh at my fellow comedians' expense. On reaching our abode it became clear that I was indeed living in dreamland as inside there was still nothing in the building in any other shade than the very familiar smoke grey.

Shortly after we had stepped next door into Tom's spotless accommodation, one of the lads swore blind that he could hear a large vehicle drawing up in the distance. We soon put this down to his imagination and forgot all about it, settling down to another evening of pointless inane conversation, fuelled by the odd beverage. Midway through one session that was bordering on the childish, my attention was drawn to a stranger who was standing outside and staring through the window at the assembled refugees. One or two of the lads reached for anything that would serve as a weapon to be used in self-defence. At that point Tom thought it best to explain to us that the peeping Tom was, in fact, at long last, the infamous agent we had been waiting so long to see. After assessing the mood of his workers by merely looking at them from a distance, he eventually saw fit to enter the building, which he did with the air of a man who had a bit more than ten quid in his pocket. A greeting and a handshake was exchanged with all the men whom he had met before and then he arrived at our corner of the room.

What Terry and myself were in Germany for was to try and earn some money, which in turn meant that we would be earning him some money – a fact that we thought should surely merit a cheery greeting. Instead his opening line was, 'So are you the intrepid explorers?' referring to our long and arduous journey through Belgium and Germany, including a night spent in a train station, all brought about by his own false information given to Terry before leaving England. Any chance he had of us forgetting the journey and actually liking the man vanished instantly and four fists clenched very tightly, while Terry headed off towards the tool bag to sort out that list of blunt instruments. We did, however, manage to restrain ourselves pretty damn quickly when it became clear that we had yet to tell him about the unit standing ten yards away from him which looked pretty normal from the outside, but was nothing more than a shell inside. My knuckles that had been clenched in anger after hearing the agent's sarcastic greeting relaxed a little and Terry soon returned from our tool bag when he realised that there wasn't a large bribe in it for us to woo our agent with.

The grimaces on our faces had already turned into fawning smiles when we took the bull by the horns and decided to reveal the damage done to our unit in its entirety to our new associate. The door swung open and I entered first, preparing to point out that it wasn't really as bad as it looked on first view. That was not an easy task, as everything inside the place was smoke grey, the curtains were sitting on the floor under the window doing a very believable impression of a nasty oil spill over the carpet and all but one of the windows had a large crack running right down the middle. I had seen the damage in all its glory more than once, but all of a sudden it seemed to look even worse than it actually was. Eventually I managed to break the ice by pointing out that the coffee machine had survived and was sitting in one of the cupboards as good as new. I quite genuinely expected that that observation would make the whole sorry situation seem just a little less serious. There was a fine line and maybe the coffee machine surviving the inferno would keep us on the safe side of it! Much to my surprise, the agent took all of two minutes to assess the situation and didn't look the slightest bit bothered. He took one more look around and told us not to worry about it and that he would clear everything up with the owners the very next day. My fawning smile turned into a cheery grin as we left the unit.

In all the confusion, Lee had moved to new digs and so when the agent declared that he would find fresh accommodation for the three of us, I mentally questioned his grasp of maths. How could Terry and myself make three? Oh well, slip of the tongue I guessed and duly forgot all about it. Surely he had made a mistake, and time would tell.

Mr Agent consumed a beer and departed early. We would all be seeing him first thing in the morning as he would be raiding his bank account in order to be able to pay us all ten days' back pay and also give Terry and me a small advance to help us through. As the day ended on a cheerful note, I could smile. Things were looking up, and it had been at least forty-eight hours since the last slap in the face... Not much longer to wait!

By the time we had set off for work the next day, the mood had changed noticeably. We were looking forward to having some money in our pockets and we would once again be sleeping in a bed that night. We almost ran all the way to work and on arrival the climb up four flights of stairs didn't seem half as bad as it usually did. I was even finding it easy to laugh at the list of gags still being fired at me about the fire. I had to get used to them as they would never stop.

Work began and we soon got stuck into it in order to ignore the constant heckling. Every time we had a break, we would again make absolutely sure that our work was duly noted for our own reference for our wage demands. Pay day was nearing and we would try to make sure that we received every pfennig due to us.

Halfway through the morning, the agent still had not arrived with the cash after promising us the evening before to be there first thing. He wasn't, so we carried on with the work, not getting too worried about it. Dinner-break arrived and the lads were beginning to get decidedly twitchy. It would not be the first time that workers abroad had been ripped off, and the agent's lateness was beginning to worry everyone. Tom quietened us all down by pointing out that since arriving some six months previously he had never received his money before 2 p.m. on pay day. By the time our break was coming to an end, the conversation was once again moving into familiar territory. The most frequently mentioned words in the last minutes of our break, as indeed they had been since our arrival in Germany, were 'insert', 'speedily' and 'power drill'. Strange feelings of *déja vu* were becoming a daily event. There was no point in becoming too angry as we still had to get the work completed in order to receive whatever the agent chose to pay us. Discussing how annoyed we all were with the whole situation wasn't going to get the work done, and so we eventually got off our arses and trekked back across to the other side of the building to continue with our tasks.

It wasn't long before our anger was replaced with eagerness as the smarmy git finally arrived with a male companion in tow. We observed closely as he wandered around the building, greeting each of his workers in turn and handing them their long-awaited wages. Finally, he reached our section of the site and greeted us politely with the stranger still tagging along and watching from a discreet distance.

The first information given us was that fresh digs had been found and that he would drive us straight there himself after work that night. Things were looking up, we dared to think – maybe prematurely. Inevitably the conversation swung in the direction of our finances. We hadn't expected the upturn in our fortunes to end quite so quickly, yet on counting the pile of notes handed to us, it came to a shuddering halt. A much smaller than expected wad of notes was handed over and I immediately rushed off to find our own calculations that had been meticulously worked out, leaving Terry to listen to the agent's obviously well-rehearsed list of reasons and excuses for his tight-fisted attitude. I returned waving our calculations, just in time to see him producing his very own. To say they differed is putting it mildly. The 'true' breakdown of costs for the work we were doing appeared from his pocket and had an impact on us like being kicked in the teeth. What he had quoted to Terry over the telephone back in England were indeed the correct prices. Unfortunately he had failed to inform us that his own slice of the action would be deducted from them before any money found its way into our pockets.

The arguments continued with our anger slowly building, whist all the time the mysterious stranger was still watching in the background. It had crossed my mind that he was probably a bodyguard as the agent must have come very close to being beaten senseless on more than one occasion. He was starting to get perilously close to it again as the next bombshell landed. The dramas we had been through such as sleeping in train stations and having to beg for money had all been brought about by him neglecting to find out for us exactly how much money we required to reach Leipzig from Zeebrugge. He had played a blinder by paying for two tickets that enabled us to get away from Frankfurt, with the promise that all expenses would be deducted in small amounts every week. Unfortunately, his interpretation of the word 'promise' was more like 'blatant lies' and so the money for the tickets, along with the small amount of money loaned, had been deducted in one large slice from our very first wage.

Needless to say, 'Thank you very much,' were not words used in the conversation that followed, especially on learning that there was even more shit flying towards the fan at pace concerning the stranger tagging along with the hated agent. We wouldn't have long to wait to discover just what form the shit would take. It would not simply be that the man in the shadows was an arsehole – we had successfully dealt with numerous examples of that phenomenon back on sites in England and were well used to them – and therefore not really a problem that couldn't be dealt with. It was the financial side that was worrying us the most.

Terry's wife and small child were waiting back home for the money to pay their bills. The family hadn't lived in luxury prior to our trip as a result of Terry's unemployment. I, myself, was waiting for the opportunity to begin to repay Lucy, to whom I owed so much money we may as well have been married. After all deductions and paying back loans, we only had one hundred and fifty pounds each in our pockets. This was just enough to live and sending money home was out of the question. It wouldn't make our respective loved ones happy, but at least we could afford to ring home that night and try our best to explain what had happened – a tough task as we were not one hundred per cent sure ourselves.

The war of words between ourselves and the agent finally came to an end after an hour, when it suddenly became apparent that absolutely nothing outside of first-degree murder was going to change our financial predicament. Then with immaculate timing, the *coup de grâce* was delivered. The stranger who had been shadowing the agent since his arrival turned out to have a name.

'This is Roger and he will be working with you from today.'

Oh super, another body to add to our disgruntled team.

Chapter Three

Let's Start Again

Clearly, three men are always going to achieve more in the space of a day's work than merely two and the wage will rise accordingly. Of course, this theory is based upon the third member of the group having the same abilities as the other two – but this was Roger! The monetary lure that Germany held had brought over thousands of greedy Brits in search of the elusive riches. Roger had gone one stage further than the rest. He had decided to travel over despite having no prior knowledge of the work he had come over to do. Terry and I had been trying with increasing desperation to find our pots of gold working as dryliners, the same capacity in which we had been working as and gaining experience in for the previous five years back on sites in Britain. Roger hadn't. He was a carpenter by trade, and therefore he didn't have the faintest idea how to do the job that he was expected to do in a professional and incredibly quick manner. Not only would he slow down our work, we would also have to split our earnings three ways. Not good and a perfect excuse to thoroughly dislike the man before he had even uttered a word.

After spending an afternoon getting to know him it was obvious that no excuses were needed. Within five minutes of talking to him it had become clear that he had nothing at all in common with either Terry or myself. Even as he was telling us about the more exciting periods of his life, the tone of his voice never changed from that you expect when hearing of a death in the family. Prolonged exposure to Roger may well result in his close family soon being informed of his own grisly demise.

Still, on the bright side, we did have some money. Our first task on the journey back to the digs that evening was to at last buy ourselves food. We felt like rich men. We could enjoy a veritable food feast, a few beers and still have enough cash left over to telephone home. The last our loved ones had known was that we were trapped in Frankfurt train station. We could now inform them that we had moved on and subsequently burned down our accommodation! It was probably best not to mention that at this early stage and so we would lie whilst trying to keep straight faces. I would tell Lucy in the hope of receiving a little sympathy and everyone else could wait.

The question of where we would be sleeping was still at the forefront of our minds, when in walked Mr Agent with joyous news. He had found us new digs, with real beds, fluffy sheets, pillows, but no cooking facilities. Time for more sandwiches. Roger would be joining us, but what the hell, we didn't care. No more sleeping on rock-solid kitchen floors for us! It was comfort all the way from now on – yeah, right. Surely we would never again be sleeping on the floor or, worse still, inside train stations. Well, not for twenty-four hours anyway.

We excitedly jumped into the agent's mobile home and began the short trip to our new residence, getting a very clear insight into how the other half lived. In the back of the vehicle there was a large comfortable bed, washing facilities, an oven, fridge and all mod cons. The agent explained to us how he would reach an agreement with a site manager who would then allow him to connect the vehicle to the site's power supply every night, enabling him to live in positive luxury compared to his serfs. He was living in Germany for approximately one tenth of what it was costing us. He would also only reveal to a chosen few the whereabouts of his vehicle at any given time, presumably to protect himself.

He dropped us off at our new digs and we waved him away, using two fingers as he drove off. Roger and Terry spotted a stall down the road selling fried chicken and so a feast was had before we sought out our new landlord, who hit us with the bad news immediately. We had a room to sleep the three of us, but only for the next two nights. From joy to despair again in ten seconds.

Our brief change of address had to be reported back to our loved ones and Lucy's cheerful tone grew fainter and fainter as I informed her of the unlikelihood of any money heading her way in the near future. The story of the fire almost finished her off. The call failed to cheer me up in any way. A friend's answering machine greeted me on the line when I made my second call, requesting name, address, message and receiving the reply, 'Andy, Germany, it's shit!'

It was still early when I vacated the telephone kiosk and so an exploration of the area began. Only yards into the trip the first watering hole appeared. Die Ocean had no signs of life and so we chose to ignore the place and head back for a good night of sleep on mattresses for a change. Another piece of the gorgeous hot chicken was purchased on the way back to the hotel and we were just about to sit back, relax and tuck in when a rap on our door spoilt the moment. Before any of us had made an attempt to get out of our chairs, a key turned in the lock and in walked the landlord with more bad news. He had been wrong earlier when he had told us that the room was ours for two nights; it would only be for one. The slaps in the face were now hurting less, as we began to expect them more.

Not surprisingly, the agent didn't show up on the site the next day. As far as he was concerned, it was a perfect situation. We were stuck, no money made, no way of getting home. He must have been rubbing his hands with glee at the thought of the commission we would earn him in our attempts to turn the situation around.

A pattern was forming. The calamities were building up and our depression slowed our work down as we hoped for something to occur that was actually beneficial to us. As we left work that day, the reality of yet another night of uneasy sleep on the floor slowly dawned. If our landlord hadn't found another bed for us, our hopes were resting on a kind relative sending us money via a travel agent operating a money transferral service – a very handy and ultimately essential form of getting your hands on some money where there is no other way.

The fact that it had come down to this after ten days of our tour was depressing to say the very least. We had had such high hopes of this trip being the point in our lives when financial roots were at long last put down. It was in actual fact becoming the exact opposite of what we had expected. Less than two weeks in and we were already borrowing yet more money in order to be able to live. However, it was about time that our luck changed. Surely our new landlord would not add to our misery by throwing us out on the street!

The knock on the door alerted us to brace ourselves for the good news that more beds had been found for us. It never came and in its place total and utter dejection set in. We were now broke, hungry and homeless. The fact that we were foreigners was only a minor point that seemed to pale in comparison to the misfortunes that were hitting us thick and fast. You know the feeling – all over the world people are dying, children are suffering, poverty and hunger are rife, yet these people have got it easy when you are going through a tiny bit of a bad patch; nobody can have it as bad as you. A load of crap, but that's human nature. We packed our bags very slowly, in the forlorn hope that in the time it took to complete the task – about two minutes – Mr Landlord would relent and return with the key to another room in his hand.

As we found the warmest kerbstone to sit our behinds on, the conversation revolved around methods of getting back to England, with the word 'stowaway' mentioned on a couple of occasions. After reaching the conclusion that this possibility was highly unlikely, ways of improving our situation in Germany was the only thing left to discuss. Half an hour of trying to find anything positive to say culminated in Terry suggesting we at least try to find a bed for the night and enquiring at Die Ocean, the friendly watering hole that we had discovered the previous evening. We walked the short distance, carrying our luggage, entered and threw the bags under a table in the far recesses of the bar area. Anyone sat in the bar with us that night, must have thought our families had been killed in a freak accident at least. One glass of beer each and total silence, our long faces only adding to the air of doom around the table.

Just as the very last drop of beer was being savoured prior to being swallowed, a long-haired stranger appeared at our table and proceeded to greet us in our native tongue. The shock of bumping into a fellow Englishman hadn't worn off before three more drinks appeared at the table, paid for out of his pocket. The few words that we had uttered since arriving had given away our nationality and the stranger had watched as we had spent an hour sinking further and further down into our seats.

'Hi, I'm John. Who's died?' was his opening line that failed to raise even a smile. He told us that he hadn't seen any Brits looking as miserable as us since the last time he had met three men who had been working for a financially ruthless agent, who after much discussion turned out to be our friend. He had seemingly made an awful lot of workers' lives a misery. We weren't the first and we would certainly not be the last. John nodded his head in time to our horror stories and even predicted one of them.

Then, partly in friendship and partly in pity, he ordered more beers and over came the barmaid, whom he began kissing and cuddling. He had been in Germany for eighteen months and lived above the place with the attractive young woman. Due to the lack of space in one room, they were not too pleased at the idea of three buddies joining them, so a bed for the night was out of the question. The dejection returned swiftly, as we prepared to use our bags as pillows and sleep anywhere for the next few days, until we at least earned the fare home.

We had thanked John for his kindness when he began to discuss the topic of work once more, mentioning that he was working directly for a German company. Whenever he was paid he received the money every week from the German foreman, removing the need to work through an agent, and cutting out the greedy middleman and pocketing all of the pay himself.

'Well, how marvellous, you lucky bastard,' was the general consensus of opinion within our team of depressed and financially challenged workers. We thanked John again for his hospitality and grabbed our bags as we prepared to leave. But John held up a hand and beckoned us to sit back down. He then proceeded to say what he had begun to explain before our jealousy took a hold. The company he was working for was short of men on the site where John worked. For some strange reason, the management believed that the Brits were the men for the job and so suitable candidates were always much sought-after. John continued by telling us where to go and who to see at five the following morning. He then wished us good luck and allowed us to leave a touch happier than if we had left earlier. Our only problem was that we still had nowhere to sleep.

It was 10 p.m. and we were about to embark upon our longest seven hours, beating even Frankfurt train station.

Our destination in the morning to meet the representative from our prospective employers was a brisk ten-minutes walk away from Leipzig train station, the biggest building in the centre of Leipzig and therefore the easiest to find. On the walk to the centre of Leipzig, our top priority was where we would be sleeping. The conclusion that we reached was obvious. Terry's and my own knowledge of sleeping in train stations plus our lack of money meant there was nowhere else. It would be a new experience for Roger, however.

Although we were facing the prospect of sleeping in our second train station in the same amount of weeks, our mood was upbeat. Hopefully we would have a new job to go to the next day and that would pay us far more than we were expecting when we had boarded that ferry. 'Mr Smarmy Git' was now in the past and nothing had been mentioned of the infamous fire. Was this a turning point?

I suppose it would have been asking too much to hope for a warm night to make our second stay within the railway stations of Germany a pleasant one. Surely we had picked the right night as it had been eighty degrees during the day.

Leipzig train station is under cover yet wide open at one end to allow the elements in. It was not to be our night as the temperature plummeted to well below zero within an hour of our arrival. The trains entering the station at that time of night were thankfully few and far between, limiting the amount of freezing blasts of wind accompanying them into the station.

Walking around the place searching for the warmest alcove was enough to keep the blood flowing until a suitable place to lay our heads was found. Eventually we found our room for the night – a ten-foot square piece of concrete outside the ladies' toilet – and we duly huddled around one cigarette lighter and made numerous attempts to sleep; not the best preparations for the interview to follow in five hours' time.

Terry and myself did eventually get some sleep whilst Roger disappeared in an attempt to find the office where the interview would take place.

When morning finally arrived, Terry and I followed Roger out of the station. Shortly after leaving the place three pairs of fingers raised angrily in unison as, by coincidence, we walked past the mobile home belonging to our agent. It was probably not a good idea to get too aggressive before we knew for certain that we would be escaping his employment, particularly while our tools were still back on his site.

An aura of 'all or nothing' filled the air as a small Portakabin bearing the company's name appeared in front of us. Terry nervously rapped on the door and a loud aggressive voice shouted out, '*Ja.*'

On entering the office a polite 'Hello' revealed our nationality and to our relief we were greeted with a broad smile, a solid, almost painful handshake and a cup of hot coffee. Not long into the meeting it was obvious that he was familiar with our circumstances and so, striking while the iron was hot, I threw John's name into the conversation at the first opportunity.

During our talk with John the previous night, he had given us the impression that he was among the more popular and trusted members of the 'Foreign Legion' currently employed by the robust gentleman in front of us, to whom we would shamelessly grovel for the duration of our 'interview'. However, the 'any friend of John's is a friend of ours' theory didn't seem to make the slightest difference to our chances of being employed. What in fact turned out to be the clincher was that we were prepared to work twelve hours a day, seven days a week. We were also prepared to appear to enjoy the slog for at least six months, or indeed, as long as he wanted us to stay.

Any commitment shown towards vast quantities of work seemed to cut more ice with the Germans than any actual ability to do the job that they would be paying you to do. At no time during our meeting with this potential employer or any other employer during the tour was any proof of our skills, either qualified or not, requested. Simply being there and appearing to know what you were doing was enough. The more people seemed to be working on the site the happier they all were. It didn't make any difference to the Germans that possibly a quarter of their foreign employees probably didn't have the faintest idea of what they were supposed to be doing. Terry and myself had Roger following us around like a lost schoolchild as proof.

Our interviewer, amazingly, didn't seem to notice the stifled chuckles coming from two areas of the office when Roger explained to him his background as a dryliner. Our prospective employer continued to sit and nod repetitively to every answer we gave in a way that made us suspect that we could have said anything at all and he would have been quite happy with the response. The language difference meant that he clearly wasn't fully aware of what we were telling him and surely there was no way on earth that it would be as easy as it was appearing to be to get employment. Yes, it could. The interview was terminated with yet another firm handshake and our new friend quoted, 'You're just the men we are looking for.'

As the relief set in we realised that we had a safe job in the hands of a reputable company who had no intention of ripping us off. It would be good to escape the clutches of a certain someone, who was clearly intent on doing just that. It was virtually impossible for the day to get any better, after he had informed the three of us that all of the British workforce on the site we were heading for had all checked into the same hotel in such numbers that any further employees of the firm would be able to check straight in without any question.

Our next task was to head back to our former site of employment to fetch our tools and inform our English agent that we no longer intended to work for the smarmy bastard. The abuse was put to one side during the walk to the site until a far more intense stream of obscenities had been agreed upon that would be more fitting for the occasion. The walk soon turned into a jog upon remembering that a hotel bed was awaiting us after putting in an appearance at our new place of work. In the short time we had been in the country we had slept on as many floors as we had beds.

The lads back on the site greeted our arrival with questions about the amount of alcohol that we had consumed the night before. There had to be a reason for us to be walking into work four and a half hours late. Keeping our cards very close to our chests, a story slowly unfolded involving beer, spirits and large amounts of debauchery! The whole tale was a tissue of lies, of course, yet a plausible excuse for our late arrival. The storytelling was received with much glee and jealousy which slowly turned into bemusement, then outright disbelief.

Concealing the truth was important as it suddenly occurred to us that revealing everything that had gone on in the previous twelve hours would put us in a very difficult situation. Had we chosen to tell our friends on the site the truth, they would have been listening to the story of how we had received a stroke of luck and how our wages would be doubling at the pastures new that we would be heading to after the farewells.

There was nothing we would have liked better than to have taken our mates along for the ride, but the building boom in the area was never going to last and whilst it was running its course there was always going to be a long queue of people such as us waiting to cash in. When we found ourselves at the front of the queue, friendship, sadly, had to take a back seat. We had no intention of arriving in the position of finding ourselves in a good job at last paying us good money, only to stand aside while all the mates we had foolishly dragged along took the work from us. Whereas, if we played dumb and pretended that we were leaving the country, we would thereby have the whole job to ourselves.

Dog eat dog – it had to be that way. In the short space of time that we had spent in the country we had already become seasoned campaigners. The journey had been an adventure itself, our employer had turned out to be a lying cheat, for various reasons mattresses had become a luxury and concrete floors felt like home. Through all of those minor problems, we had, however, managed to find another job ourselves and had no intention at all of giving it away.

We gathered the tools that we had returned to the site to collect and all of the lads had bid us farewell when, with perfect timing, in walked our by then ex-employer. With his stuffed wallet in one hand and his mobile phone in the other, he greeted the rest of the lads and then turned to see Terry, myself and Roger standing, doing precisely nothing and so he hurriedly made his way over us. He may not have had much, but what he did possess was a trained eye when it came to spotting no commission being earned for him. (Possibly only a quarter of what we had earned would leave his pocket and make its way into ours.)

I am not sure our opening line of, 'Hello, we'll be off now,' was quite what he had been expecting. His enquiry about whether we were taking the afternoon off was met with the answer, 'Yes, and every other afternoon, you git.'

This did not seem to go down too well and when he asked us why we were leaving, the torrent of abuse was long and ferocious. It felt good, very good.

When he realised that we were not joking he decided it was time to show his true colours, the subject of the inferno came into the conversation with him promising us that he would do nothing at all to deflect the flak that would inevitably come our way in the not too distant future. We didn't care. We were confident and duly ignored everything he said, finally making our way out of the building. One particularly nasty chapter of our tour had come to an end and with it we had severed all ties with one of the most disliked men in the country – and he wasn't even German.

Smiles appeared on our faces as we left the building for the very last time. We threw our tools into the back of a taxi parked outside and made the one-mile journey to our next work site.

The site was not the usual large, open and very muddy plot of land being developed. It was an old building that looked like it could tell a few stories about the city's past, and not many of them good. As a reward for its long service it was receiving a well-earned facelift. It was surrounded from top to bottom with scaffolding, but fortunately for us it was clear that not only the face of the building was being lifted, but the interior was getting the same treatment.

We wandered in, bellowing John's name, to the amusement of the twenty or thirty men working away inside. Countless steps on a winding staircase led us up to the fourth floor where John's familiar face at last appeared. He was fully aware of where we had slept the previous night and was genuinely pleased to see us arrive at the site. Accommodation for him was no problem due to his 'arrangement' back at the drinking den where we had first met and he introduced us to one of his fellow workers who pointed us in the direction of the hotel where the rest of the Brits on the site were staying.

Our tools were quickly stowed away safely until the next day as a good night's sleep was priority number one. We could check straight into the hotel and wouldn't have to pay for a week, due to the company's arrangement with the hotel management. So many men from the firm had booked in and paid their bills regularly that the hotel had extended some trust in their direction, a rare luxury in the city at that time.

Our arrival at the hotel was greeted by blank faces. They had definitely not been expecting us. One mention of our employer's name, though, and their arms opened wide. The hotel had agreed to cut everybody's weekly bill due to the sheer volume of custom that we were providing, and our bill would get steadily smaller with every new face we in turn pointed in the hotel's direction. Every British worker staying there knew an endless supply of his fellow countrymen and they in turn each knew another supply, etc. The agreement seemed ideal. In no time at all the building would be full of useful contacts for us and we would all be living there for almost nothing. It was perfect and we hadn't even seen the room yet.

The key turned in the lock and we stepped into paradise. Three decent beds, comfortable chairs, television with satellite stations that picked up English-speaking channels and a strange plastic appliance in the kitchen that heated up water to make hot drinks. I vaguely remembered using one back in England and immediately set about making a celebratory pot of tea to mark our good fortune. Surely all this was too good to be true, and it would only be a matter of time before we took the next slap in the face!

A search through the television channels produced a party-like atmosphere in the room. It was football World Cup time and we found a channel dedicated to the subject that the hotel had been delightful enough to tune in for us. Terry and Roger began furiously shaking me by the hand in a rare show of friendship and thanked me for burning down that cheap set of digs. The three of us soon came to the conclusion that there had been no need to panic in those hours following the inferno as the owner would surely now see that the lack of a satellite system meant that the building and all its contents deserved to perish. If I had not forgotten about those trotter burgers that I had thrown into the makeshift deep-fat fryer, we would still be working for Beelzebub himself, we would have no new job to look forward to and we would not have been sitting in comfort enjoying a pot of tea and watching the football. Maybe it was fate. The previous few days had all been a nightmare but now we were back in the real world.

As I filled a bath to the brim with hot soapy water, I pondered on how good life had become, quite literally overnight. It was to become even better, as we were to discover in an hour's time when exploring the premises. The restaurant at the hotel was serving hot food that we could actually afford. Our standard of living had risen and we decided to abandon our staple diet of toast, eggs and trotter burgers. That night would be different. We would sit down and use knives and forks to eat what could be described as a decent meal for the first time in Germany. After a week of eating pieces of chicken, tuna, salad, etc., you suddenly realise that you cannot remember the last time you ate something that was anything other than lukewarm – a fitting punishment for overdoing those Frikadelle quite so intensely on that infamous night.

The word 'restaurant' is usually applied to an eating establishment, but for us it symbolised a magnet whose field we were drawn into and could not, and had no intention of, escaping. I was still slightly damp from my bath when we happily sat around what was shortly to become 'our table'. The three of us took a look at the menu and realised that the tastier dishes on offer were well out of our price range. For that reason, along with our inability to understand most of it, three spaghetti bolognaise were duly ordered and greedily consumed.

The adventure that was Germany had come full circle in the space of forty-eight hours. A few days previously it was a case of total despair as Terry and myself tried to think of any way possible to get home other than stowing away. Even that possibility would have soon become a realistic proposition had I continued on my mission to leave half of Leipzig in ashes! Instead we were about to leave a restaurant stuffed to the gills and thoroughly content with life.

It was still only ten hours since we had staggered out of the train station. Exhaustion was beginning to take a hold. It is strange how thoughts of sleep vanish when you have access to a TV station that speaks your language in a country that does not. Back at our room, the comfortable furniture possessed the same magnetic qualities as the restaurant and our backsides were stuck to the cushions! A cheap and tasteless packet of cigarettes found their way on to the arm of my chair, the television came to life and the most energetic activity undertaken during the rest of that night were the trips to and from the kitchen area to make endless pots of tea.

Terry eventually grew tired of the all-night pop videos and got up to find what would become his bed. Five minutes later, Roger and myself also found our respective beds and within seconds a bomb could have struck the hotel and not one of us would have stirred. Had the explosion been powerful enough to wake us from our slumber, none of us would have cared anyway.

Perfection eventually came to an end at 7 a.m. when Terry woke us up and pointed out that we should have shown our faces on the site an hour previously. Our late arrival on day one of the new job would do us no favours at all. Clothing was quite literally thrown on and we made the short walk to the tram stop, swapping insults and blaming one another for the sloppy timekeeping. A long and complex tissue of lies was rehearsed that would serve as our excuse on meeting the foreman.

The foreman on the site, Thomas, was the first to welcome us on our late arrival and listened with interest to our story of disorientation in our new surroundings – wrong trams being caught and every clichéd excuse in the 'late for work' handbook. Fortunately, Thomas was an instantly likeable man who gave us the impression that he couldn't give a damn whether we were late or not. There was method behind his madness. We would only be paid for the work we did and so if we failed to turn up, it was our loss and not his. Thomas turned a blind eye to our instantly forgettable tale and led us around the building, pointing out the work that we had been allocated and explaining that all the rooms above ground floor were to be private apartments, nothing spectacular, just comfortable dwellings.

Leipzig hadn't got a housing problem; communism made sure of that. Everyone had a home. The vast majority of the city's population were living in what appeared to all of the Westerners to be old, damp and certainly not aesthetically pleasing buildings. When we stood back and thought, we couldn't remember the last private residence that we had seen that wasn't in one large block of identical units. A place to live with any degree of luxury would sell, and quickly. Capitalism had come to the East!

Thomas had a command of English but not one great enough to explain the finer details of the work we were to be doing. John, our saviour, took over the reins and congratulated us on our very late arrival. Then, before any discussion surrounding trivial matters such as work, we were introduced to the rest of the British lads on the site.

Had we sat down the previous evening and compiled a list of differing personalities that we would expect to find on the site, we would have found it extremely difficult to invent a more diverse range than the one we met that day and went on to share the same workspace with for the next six months. It consisted of the customary pair of alcoholics working to pay for their beer, an ex-con only released a month before and there to make a fresh start, while all the time offering to 'acquire' cheap televisions, videos, etc. The playboy was also there who had exhausted his supply of females back in Britain and had decided to try his luck on the continent. Finally, there were one or two characters who were simply normal guys trying to earn an honest living in a foreign land after the opportunities at home had dried up. All of our new-found workmates seemed cheerful enough and came across as glad to have fresh faces to talk to. There was no time for petty disagreements – they were pointless and made an already difficult situation a lot more uncomfortable. However, arguing is a realistic release from constantly being nice to each other, so any new bodies on the site were always welcomed, purely for a change of conversation.

After our introductions, John returned to his work and we set off to have a good look around the site on our own, to get a more thorough idea of what needed to be done. We had already been shown the entire building by Thomas but hadn't been paying much attention to the work that was awaiting us in each room.

The first room we entered was not one of those ear-marked for work to be done inside – just as well! It was as if any refuse collected since the site had opened had been thrown into that one room. An oil drum had been placed right in the middle of the room to act as a makeshift dustbin. A good idea, if only someone had seen fit to empty it when it had become full. Strewn around everywhere were empty cigarette packets, half-eaten sandwiches, used tissue paper, rotten food, beer bottles and all manner of rotting, stinking garbage. It was difficult to believe that anybody could let the place get so disgusting and not even care.

We were standing in the Brits' tea room! Every single building site in Britain has a place exactly like that one. The last thing on your mind when consuming your food and drink in a derelict building is keeping the place tidy. As soon as the work is completed, all of the builders move out and some other unfortunate individual gets to clean up the mess. It's a harsh world.

The only different thing about this particular five-star canteen that we could see was the sheer volume of empty beer cans rolling around under our feet and standing proudly on the floor, the chairs, the window ledges, in fact anywhere it was possible to store an empty metal can. They were, quite clearly, not merely the remains left by a sly duo taking a break and slipping off quietly for a crafty couple of drinks. A walk five yards down the corridor to the room next door made the reason for the debris clear, pretty damn quick.

In disbelief, I and the two other shocked newcomers glanced down at our watches. It was 10.30 – two hours to dinner-break. Trying to translate German is not the easiest thing to achieve when you haven't had a single lesson in your whole life. The procedure becomes almost impossible when you are struggling to understand what is being said by a group of Germans who are, not to put too fine a point on it, pissed as rats! We had stumbled across the German tea room. The room next door had become too filthy for even their Teutonic tastes. To save them an entire afternoon cleaning it up, they had simply moved next door and handed the area over to us Brits!

Somewhere amongst that drunken mass were men in charge of erecting scaffolding, staircases and other potentially lethal objects that we would be placing our fragile bodies on top of. Some poor sod is going to get hurt one day, I thought. I should have been a fortune teller.

The actual work we were to be doing differed only slightly from what we were used to and so proved to be easy enough. We were, however, still having to teach Roger everything we knew. There was one small area of the work that neither Terry nor myself had ever tried and so we sent Roger off to watch the work being done, fully expecting him to be an expert by the end of the day. Fabulous – extra money and, more importantly, we had got rid of the man for a bit. He had spent the final days back on the first site realising that he didn't have a clue what he was doing and complaining incessantly about everything, coming within an inch of being murdered on numerous occasions.

Ten hours passed and 'our table' was beckoning us at the restaurant in the hotel. We scrubbed up in double-quick time and made our way to the feast. Walking through the door, I held up three fingers and muttered, 'Spag boll,' to the waiter who had served us the previous evening. The plates were soon in front of us and the food upon them even sooner inside us. A satisfactory excuse for not tipping had to be found before we departed. That time, it was to be the waiter's dreadful beige suit, as we claimed to have been put off our food by its very appearance.

The final hours of the day were once again spent glued to the television and it was still on to awaken us the following morning. Outside it was hot, very hot. Three pairs of shorts appeared and very English, milk-white legs were about to make their way to work, being heartily laughed at by the entire city of Leipzig. Surely some thanks would have been more appropriate, due to the extra tan they all got from the sun reflecting off our limbs!

Before braving the stifling heat though, the receptionist had called out my name as we made our way outside. She was holding up an envelope bearing an English stamp. I took the letter and opened it, whereupon I recognised Lucy's handwriting instantly. The last contact I had had with her before that morning was after the fire. I was still in a state of panic then and hadn't had a great deal to tell her in my subdued state. No problem – she would understand and have plenty of news to tell me and put a smile on my face. Wrong! All three of my chins struck the floor on opening the envelope and reading the opening passage. 'You stupid, stupid bastard! I can't see me ever getting my money back.'

Other pleasantries – sorry, obscenities – followed as I developed yet another chin which swiftly followed its partners down to the floor. Halfway through the letter, annoyance took a grip and the remainder found its way into the nearest bin. I knew it was only her way of discussing things and, after all, it was actually true. I had been very, very stupid. But my mother had been married at the time of my birth! Nevertheless, the writing was now on the wall.

After our arrival at the site the work began, as Terry and I had agreed, with us telling Roger to piss off and learn everything that it was feasibly possible to learn in the shortest time he could. We had three weeks of the tour left before taking our first break and the trip back to England. The work that Roger could manage to do without being chained to myself and Terry would go a long way towards us returning home with some semblance of pride after the financial disasters of the previous weeks. We just wanted to spend the next working weeks keeping our heads down, doing an awful lot of work and having the occasional laugh with the lads.

Terry volunteered to do the paperwork required by the firm in order for us to receive any money for the work that we had done. After just one week, we were beginning to like the look of what we saw in the 'total' column, although our delight was tempered by the deductions after tossing a third of the share Roger's way.

Top: 1994 - Glyn, Team B and an impatient foreman.
Middle: 1994 - The infamous building site/quagmire.
Bottom: 1994 - On the site.

Top: 1997 - Andy and Christian hit the town.
Middle: 1997 - One for the road, Romy?
Bottom: 1994 - George and Terry - smile please.